# Plant-Based Instant Pot Cookbook for Beginners

150 Electric Pressure Cooker Recipes for Everyday Cooking. Elevate Your Vegan Lifestyle with Quick, Nutrient-packed Meals

# Table of Contents

# Benefits of a Plant-Based Diet

In recent years, the popularity of plant-based diets has surged as people become increasingly conscious of their health, the environment, and animal welfare. A plant-based diet involves consuming predominantly plant-derived foods while minimizing or eliminating animal products. This shift in dietary choices has been met with widespread enthusiasm, not just from vegans and vegetarians but also from individuals seeking a healthier and more sustainable lifestyle. The benefits of a plant-based diet extend far beyond personal well-being, encompassing environmental and ethical considerations as well.

One of the primary advantages of adopting a plant-based diet is its positive impact on heart health. Numerous studies have shown that plant-based diets can reduce the risk of cardiovascular diseases. The high fiber content, coupled with the absence of saturated fats found in many animal products, helps lower cholesterol levels and maintain healthy blood pressure. A diet rich in fruits, vegetables, whole grains, and nuts contributes to improved cardiovascular function, reducing the likelihood of heart-related issues.

Plant-based diets are often associated with effective weight management and weight loss. The emphasis on nutrient-dense, low-calorie foods means individuals can enjoy satisfying meals while consuming fewer overall calories. Additionally, plant-based diets are typically higher in fiber, promoting feelings of fullness and reducing the likelihood of overeating. This can be particularly beneficial for those looking to achieve or maintain a healthy weight.

Research consistently suggests that a plant-based diet is linked to a reduced risk of various chronic diseases, including type 2 diabetes, certain cancers, and hypertension. The abundance of antioxidants, vitamins, and minerals found in plant-based foods strengthens the immune system and supports overall health, creating a natural defense against chronic conditions.

A plant-based diet is inherently rich in dietary fiber, promoting optimal digestive health. Fiber aids in maintaining regular bowel movements, preventing constipation, and fostering a healthy gut microbiome. A balanced and diverse plant-based diet encourages the growth of beneficial bacteria in the digestive tract, contributing to improved digestion and nutrient absorption.

Beyond personal health benefits, choosing a plant-based diet can have a positive impact on the environment. Animal agriculture is a significant contributor to deforestation, water pollution, and greenhouse gas emissions. By opting for plant-based alternatives, individuals can reduce their ecological footprint, conserve water, and mitigate the environmental impact associated with industrial animal farming.

For many individuals, the decision to adopt a plant-based diet is rooted in ethical considerations regarding the treatment of animals. Choosing plant-based foods helps decrease the demand for animal products, leading to reduced reliance on factory farming practices. This aligns with a growing societal awareness of animal welfare issues and supports a more compassionate approach to food consumption.

The benefits of a plant-based diet extend far beyond the confines of personal health, encompassing environmental sustainability and ethical considerations. By embracing a diet rich in fruits, vegetables, whole grains, and legumes, individuals can enhance their well-being while contributing to a healthier planet. Whether motivated by health concerns, environmental consciousness, or ethical principles, the shift toward plant-based living represents a positive step toward a more sustainable and compassionate future.

# Embracing a Plant-Based Lifestyle

In a contemporary world increasingly valuing health-conscious choices and sustainable living, the plant-based lifestyle has emerged as a powerful and transformative choice. Whether driven by health considerations, environmental consciousness, or ethical beliefs, adopting a plant-based diet can be a fulfilling and rewarding journey. To guide you through this lifestyle change, we present an extensive set of tips to help you embrace a plant-based diet with confidence and ease.

*Educate Yourself on Nutrition.* Commence your plant-based journey by delving deep into the understanding of the nutritional requirements of your body. Immerse yourself in the knowledge of essential nutrients found in plant-based foods and how to achieve a well-balanced diet. Familiarize yourself with sources of protein, iron, calcium, vitamin B12, and omega-3 fatty acids in the vast array of plant offerings.

*Gradual Transition.* A gradual transition can be more sustainable and comfortable, acting as a gentle introduction to the world of plant-based eating. Begin by incorporating one or two plant-based meals into your week, and progressively elevate the frequency as you become more accustomed to the lifestyle. This measured approach allows for a smoother adjustment, both for your evolving taste buds and your digestive system.

*Diversify Your Plate.* Embark on a culinary adventure by exploring the incredible variety of plant-based foods available. From the rainbow hues of vibrant fruits and vegetables to the heartiness of whole grains, legumes, nuts, and seeds, diversifying your plate ensures a broad spectrum of nutrients and keeps your meals exciting, enticing both your palate and your senses.

*Optimize Plant-Based Protein Sources.* Ensure you meet your protein requirements by strategically incorporating a diverse range of plant-based protein sources. From the humble beans and lentils to the versatile tofu, tempeh, quinoa, and edamame, enrich your meals with a mosaic of proteins. Combining different protein sources throughout the day helps ensure a complete amino acid profile, supporting your body's needs.

*Prioritize Whole Foods.* Elevate your commitment to health by placing a premium on whole, minimally processed foods. Let whole grains, fresh fruits, vegetables, and legumes take center stage, providing not only essential vitamins, minerals, and fiber but also contributing to a sense of satiety and sustained energy throughout the day.

*Mindful Nutrient Intake.* While a plant-based diet is inherently rich in nutrients, adopt a proactive stance by paying careful attention to specific vitamins and minerals that may require additional consideration. Consider incorporating supplements for nutrients like vitamin B12, vitamin D, and omega-3 fatty acids, which may be less abundant in plant-based diets.

*Strategic Meal Planning.* Navigate your culinary journey with foresight by strategically planning your meals. Craft a diverse menu that seamlessly integrates a mix of protein sources, a vibrant array of colorful vegetables, wholesome whole grains, and nourishing healthy fats. Preparing meals in advance not only saves time but also reduces the likelihood of opting for less healthy, convenience-driven choices.

*Label Reading Awareness.* Develop a keen eye for label scrutiny to identify any hidden animal products or undesirable additives. Cultivate familiarity with alternative names for animal-derived ingredients, empowering yourself to make informed and conscious choices while navigating the aisles of packaged foods. Your commitment to label reading ensures your dietary choices align with your plant-based principles.

*Hydration is Key.* Amplify your well-being by staying adequately hydrated through intentional consumption of water-rich fruits and vegetables, invigorating herbal teas, and refreshing infused water. Proper hydration is a cornerstone of digestive health, nutrient absorption, and overall vitality, ensuring you are poised to thrive in your plant-based lifestyle.

*Connect with the Plant-Based Community.* Elevate your journey by forging connections with a supportive community. Engage with like-minded individuals through vibrant social media groups, attend local meetups, or participate in online forums. Sharing experiences, triumphs, and tips with others on a similar journey not only fosters a sense of community but also enriches your plant-based experience, making the transition more enjoyable and sustainable.

Adopting a plant-based lifestyle transcends a mere dietary shift; it's a holistic approach to well-being that can positively impact your health, the environment, and animal welfare. By immersing yourself in education, embracing a gradual transition, and staying mindful of your nutritional needs, you can embark on this transformative journey with confidence and experience the manifold benefits of a plant-powered life.

# Instant Pot Using Tips

The Instant Pot has revolutionized home cooking, offering convenience without compromising flavor. To make the most of this versatile kitchen appliance, here are essential tips that will elevate your Instant Pot culinary adventures.

Understanding the nuanced art of cooking times is where the true prowess of the Instant Pot emerges. This multifaceted kitchen appliance isn't just a time-saver; it's a culinary game-changer. Delving into the intricacies of how quickly the Instant Pot can transform ingredients opens the door to efficient, flavorful, and stress-free cooking experiences. The Instant Pot operates with precision, significantly reducing the time needed for traditional cooking methods. Whether you're preparing grains, meats, or legumes, being mindful of the accelerated cooking times is key to achieving consistent and delightful results. To harness the time-saving potential, familiarize yourself with how the Instant Pot handles various ingredients. Grains may cook swiftly, while tougher cuts of meat might require a bit more time under pressure. This adaptability allows you to tailor your approach based on the nature of the dish.

Maintaining an adequate liquid level in the Instant Pot is paramount for successful pressure cooking. The Instant Pot relies on liquid, typically water or broth, to generate steam and build pressure. This pressurized environment is what significantly reduces cooking times, making it essential for the proper functioning of the pressure cooking process. Ensuring there's enough liquid in the pot helps prevent burn errors. The Instant Pot's sensors detect when the temperature is rising too quickly, signaling a potential issue. Sufficient liquid acts as a buffer, preventing the ingredients from sticking to the bottom and triggering the burn warning. Liquid facilitates even heat distribution throughout the pot, ensuring that all ingredients receive consistent and thorough cooking. This is especially important when preparing dishes with multiple components, as it helps avoid unevenly cooked or undercooked sections. In the absence of adequate liquid, there's a risk of scorching or burning, particularly during the Saute function or when pressure cooking ingredients prone to sticking. Sufficient liquid acts as a protective layer, preventing this and preserving the integrity of your dish. The right amount of liquid also contributes to the texture of your final dish. It helps maintain moisture levels, preventing overcooking and ensuring that proteins stay tender while grains and vegetables retain their desired consistency. Proper pressurization ensures a safe and effective pressure release when cooking is complete. Inadequate liquid levels may interfere with the release process, potentially leading to undercooked food or safety concerns.

Understanding when to use natural release versus quick release in the Instant Pot is key to achieving optimal results, especially for delicate foods. Delicate foods such as fish, grains, and certain vegetables benefit from natural release. Allowing the pressure to subside gradually prevents rapid temperature changes that can affect the texture and integrity of sensitive ingredients. Natural release reduces the likelihood of hot liquids spattering, which is particularly important when dealing with dishes that have a higher liquid content. Quick release is suitable for recipes with shorter cooking times, like many grains and vegetables. It rapidly reduces pressure, allowing you to open the Instant Pot sooner. For certain vegetables, quick release helps preserve a crisp texture by halting the cooking process promptly. This is advantageous when aiming for a balance between tenderness and firmness. In some recipes, a combination of natural and quick release may be appropriate. For example, a natural release followed by a quick release can offer the benefits of both methods, providing gentle pressure reduction without prolonged cooking times. Always consult your recipe for specific release instructions. Recipes often indicate whether natural or quick release is preferred based on the nature of the ingredients and the desired outcome. oods with a high starch content, like rice or pasta, may foam during quick release. Exercise caution to avoid clogging the steam release valve. It's often recommended to wait a few minutes before initiating a quick release for such dishes.

Strategic layering of ingredients in the Instant Pot is a smart approach that enhances even cooking and maximizes flavor integration. Placing denser items at the bottom ensures that they receive more direct contact with the heat source. This is particularly beneficial for proteins or hard vegetables, allowing them to cook thoroughly and contribute to the overall texture of the dish. Layering ingredients strategically promotes the mingling of flavors. As liquids and aromatics from the lower layers rise during cooking, they infuse the ingredients above, creating a harmonious blend of tastes throughout the dish. By arranging ingredients based on their density and cooking times, you reduce the risk of overcooking lighter, more delicate components while waiting for denser items to cook through. This thoughtful layering helps maintain the integrity of each element. Optimizing the arrangement of ingredients allows you to make the most of the Instant Pot's capacity. You can cook multiple components simultaneously without sacrificing evenness in cooking. Be mindful of the cooking times required for different ingredients. Place those with longer cooking times closer to the bottom to ensure they receive sufficient heat, while quicker-cooking items can be layered on top. Liquids naturally settle at the bottom, so positioning denser ingredients there allows them to absorb flavors more effectively. This contributes to a well-rounded taste in the final dish. The Instant Pot's ability to cook multiple ingredients in one pot is a time-saving advantage. Strategic layering enhances this convenience by allowing you to create complex, multi-component meals with minimal effort. If stacking ingredients, ensure that the top layer is not too densely packed to allow for proper steam circulation. This helps maintain consistent cooking conditions throughout the Instant Pot.

Respecting the recommended maximum fill line on your Instant Pot is crucial for ensuring both safety and optimal performance. The maximum fill line is designed to prevent overfilling, which could compromise the Instant Pot's ability to generate and maintain the necessary pressure for cooking. Respecting this limit ensures that the pressure release system functions as intended, contributing to safe and effective cooking. Overfilling the Instant Pot increases the risk of ingredients, especially liquids, reaching the steam release valve. This can lead to clogging, hindering the release of pressure during and after cooking. Adhering to the fill line minimizes this risk, promoting the smooth operation of the steam release valve. Overfilling the Instant Pot can pose safety hazards, such as excessive pressure buildup or potential leaks. Respecting the fill line guidelines mitigates these risks, creating a safer cooking environment. Following the recommended fill line helps maintain proper liquid-to-ingredient ratios, contributing to even cooking. Balanced proportions of ingredients and liquid are essential for achieving desired textures and flavors in your dishes.

Regularly cleaning the sealing ring in your Instant Pot is a small yet impactful practice for maintaining the freshness of your dishes. The sealing ring can absorb odors from the foods you've cooked. Regular cleaning helps eliminate any lingering smells, preventing unwanted flavor transfers between different dishes prepared in the Instant Pot. A clean sealing ring ensures that the aromas and flavors of each dish remain true to their original profiles. This is particularly important when transitioning from savory to sweet dishes or when preparing recipes with distinct flavor profiles. Some dishes, especially strongly flavored ones, can leave residual tastes in the sealing ring. Cleaning prevents these flavors from carrying over into subsequent dishes, allowing each meal to stand on its own in terms of taste and aroma.

Ensuring the float valve in your Instant Pot moves freely is a vital maintenance step for optimal performance and safety. The float valve is a crucial component in regulating pressure within the Instant Pot. It rises and falls with pressure changes during the cooking process. Regular cleaning ensures that it moves freely, allowing for accurate pressure adjustments and maintaining a safe cooking environment. Over time, food particles and residue can accumulate around the float valve, hindering its movement. Regular cleaning prevents blockages, ensuring that the valve can operate smoothly. This is particularly important for maintaining consistent pressure levels during cooking. A float valve that is obstructed or doesn't move freely can lead to pressure build-up problems. This may result in safety concerns, including the potential for the Instant Pot not functioning as intended or difficulty in releasing pressure after cooking. Regular maintenance, including cleaning the float valve, helps prolong the lifespan of your Instant Pot. By preventing issues with pressure build-up, you contribute to the overall longevity and reliability of the appliance.

Consult your Instant Pot's manual for model-specific guidance and always be open to experimentation. With these tips, you'll confidently navigate the world of Instant Pot cooking, creating effortless and delicious meals. Happy Instant Pot adventures!

Foundational
Broths &
Bases

# Hearty Vegetable Broth

## INGREDIENTS

**Ingredients:**

- 2 large carrots, roughly chopped
- 2 celery stalks, roughly chopped
- 1 large onion, peeled and quartered
- 4 garlic cloves, smashed
- 1 medium-sized leek, cleaned and chopped (white and light green parts only)
- 2 bay leaves
- 1 tsp whole black peppercorns
- 6 cups of water
- 1 small bunch of fresh parsley, thyme

 Prep Time: 15 min

 Cook Time: 30 minutes

 Serves: 4

## DIRECTIONS

Place all the vegetables, herbs, and spices into the Instant Pot. Add water, ensuring you don't go past the maximum fill line. Lock the Instant Pot lid in place and set the valve to the sealing position. Select the "Soup/Broth" setting and adjust the time to 30 minutes at high pressure. Once the cooking time is over, let the pressure release naturally for 15 minutes, then carefully turn the valve to venting for a quick release. Strain the broth through a fine-mesh sieve into a large bowl or pot, discarding the solids. Store in airtight containers in the fridge or freeze for future use.

## NUTRITIONAL INFORMATION

Per serving: approx. 40 calories, 1g protein, 10g carbohydrates, 0.2g fat, 2.5g fiber, 0mg cholesterol, 290mg sodium, 300mg potassium.

# Miso Ginger Base

## INGREDIENTS

- 4 tbsp white miso paste (ensure it's plant-based; some varieties might have fish additives)
- 1 large piece (about 2 inches) of fresh ginger, peeled and thinly sliced
- 4 garlic cloves, minced
- 1 onion, chopped
- 2 tbsp soy sauce or tamari
- 4 cups of water
- 2 green onions, chopped (for garnish)
- 1 tbsp sesame oil
- 1 tsp chili flakes (optional)

 Prep Time: 10 min

 Cook Time: 20 minute

 Serves: 4

## DIRECTIONS

Set the Instant Pot to "Sauté" mode. Add the sesame oil, followed by onions, ginger, and garlic. Sauté until the onions are translucent and the ginger and garlic are fragrant. Add the miso paste and stir until it's dissolved in the sautéed mixture. Pour in the water and soy sauce (or tamari). Mix well, ensuring there are no lumps of miso paste remaining. Lock the Instant Pot lid in place, set the valve to the sealing position, and select "Soup/Broth" setting for 20 minutes.

Once done, allow for a natural release for 10 minutes and then turn the valve for a quick release. Strain if desired, and garnish with green onions before serving.

## NUTRITIONAL INFORMATION

Per serving: approx. 85 calories, 3g protein, 12g carbohydrates, 3g fat, 1.5g fiber, 0mg cholesterol, 820mg sodium, 185mg potassium.

# Aromatic Tomato Puree

## INGREDIENTS

- 8 ripe tomatoes, quartered
- 1 medium onion, chopped
- 4 garlic cloves, minced
- 2 tbsp olive oil
- 1 tsp dried basil
- 1 tsp dried oregano
- 1/2 tsp sea salt (or to taste)
- 1/4 tsp black pepper
- 1/2 cup fresh basil leaves (optional, for enhanced flavor)
- 2 cups of water

 Prep Time: 15 min

 Cook Time: 25 minutes

 Serves: 4

## DIRECTIONS

Set the Instant Pot to "Sauté" mode. Add olive oil, followed by onions and garlic. Sauté until the onions are translucent. Add the quartered tomatoes, dried basil, dried oregano, salt, and pepper. Stir well, allowing the flavors to meld for a couple of minutes. Pour in the water and mix. If using, add the fresh basil leaves. Lock the Instant Pot lid in place, set the valve to the sealing position, and select "Pressure Cook" or "Manual" setting for 25 minutes. Once done, allow for a natural release. Blend the mixture using an immersion blender or transfer to a blender to achieve a smooth puree consistency.

## NUTRITIONAL INFORMATION

Per serving: 90 calories, 2g protein, 12g carbohydrates, 4.5g fat, 3g fiber, 0mg cholesterol, 320mg sodium, 450mg potassium.

# Creamy Cashew Sauce Base

## INGREDIENTS

- 1.5 cups raw cashews, soaked for 4 hours or overnight
- 2 cups water
- 4 garlic cloves
- 1 tbsp lemon juice
- 1 tbsp nutritional yeast (optional, for a cheesy flavor)
- 1/2 tsp sea salt (or to taste)
- 1/4 tsp black pepper
- 1/2 tsp onion powder

 Prep Time: 4 hours (for soaking) + 10 minutes

 Cook Time: 10 minutes

 Serves: 4

## DIRECTIONS

Start by draining and rinsing the soaked cashews. Place cashews, water, garlic cloves, lemon juice, nutritional yeast (if using), salt, pepper, and onion powder into the Instant Pot. Lock the Instant Pot lid in place, set the valve to the sealing position, and select "Manual" or "Pressure Cook" setting for 10 minutes on low pressure. Once done, allow for a natural release for about 10 minutes, then use the quick release for any remaining pressure. Blend the mixture using an immersion blender or carefully transfer to a blender until a smooth and creamy consistency is achieved.

## NUTRITIONAL INFORMATION

Per serving: 265 calories, 8g protein, 17g carbohydrates, 20g fat, 2g fiber, 0mg cholesterol, 320mg sodium, 320mg potassium.

# Nutty Almond Broth

## INGREDIENTS

- 1 cup raw almonds
- 6 cups water
- 1 onion, chopped
- 3 garlic cloves, minced
- 1 bay leaf
- 1 tsp sea salt (or to taste)
- 1/4 tsp black pepper
- 2 tbsp olive oil
- 1 sprig of fresh rosemary (optional)

 Prep Time: 10 minutes

 Cook Time: 40 minutes

 Serves: 4

## DIRECTIONS

In the Instant Pot, set it to "Sauté" mode. Add the olive oil, followed by the chopped onion. Sauté until translucent. Add the minced garlic and sauté for an additional 2 minutes. Add the raw almonds, water, bay leaf, salt, and pepper (and rosemary if using) to the pot. Lock the Instant Pot lid in place, set the valve to the sealing position, and select the "Soup/Broth" setting for 40 minutes. Once the cook time is over, allow for a natural pressure release. Strain the broth through a fine-mesh sieve, discarding the solids.

## NUTRITIONAL INFORMATION

Per serving: 125 calories, 4g protein, 7g carbohydrates, 10g fat, 3g fiber, 0mg cholesterol, 590mg sodium, 175mg potassium.

# Lemon Herb Infusion

## INGREDIENTS

- 4 cups water
- Peel of 2 lemons (avoid the white pith as it can be bitter)
- 1 sprig fresh rosemary
- 2 sprigs fresh thyme
- 2 sprigs fresh mint
- 1 tbsp agave nectar or maple syrup (optional, for sweetness)

  Prep Time: 5 min

 Cook Time: 15 minutes

 Serves: 4

## DIRECTIONS

Add the water, lemon peel, rosemary, thyme, and mint to the Instant Pot. Lock the Instant Pot lid in place, set the valve to the sealing position, and select the "Manual" or "Pressure Cook" setting for 15 minutes on low pressure. Once the cooking time is over, quick release the pressure. Remove and discard the herbs and lemon peels. Stir in the agave nectar or maple syrup if desired. Serve the infusion hot or let it cool and refrigerate for a refreshing cold drink.

## NUTRITIONAL INFORMATION

Per serving: 20 calories, 0g protein, 5g carbohydrates, 0g fat, 0g fiber, 0mg cholesterol, 5mg sodium, 30mg potassium.

# Coconut Curry Base

## INGREDIENTS

- 1 can (13.5 oz) full-fat coconut milk
- 2 tbsp curry powder
- 1 medium onion, finely chopped
- 3 garlic cloves, minced
- 1 tbsp ginger, grated
- 1 tbsp olive oil or coconut oil
- 1 tsp turmeric powder
- 1/2 tsp cumin powder
- 1 tsp sea salt (or to taste)
- 1/4 tsp black pepper
- 2 cups vegetable broth

Prep Time: 10 min

Cook Time: 20 minutes

Serves: 4

## DIRECTIONS

Turn on the Instant Pot's "Sauté" mode. Add the oil, followed by the onions, garlic, and ginger. Sauté until the onions become translucent. Stir in the curry powder, turmeric, cumin, salt, and pepper. Cook for 2 minutes to allow the spices to release their flavors. Pour in the coconut milk and vegetable broth. Mix well, ensuring there are no dry spices sticking to the bottom of the pot. Lock the Instant Pot lid in place, set the valve to the sealing position, and select "Pressure Cook" or "Manual" setting for 20 minutes. Once done, quick release the pressure.

## NUTRITIONAL INFORMATION

Per serving: 240 calories, 3g protein, 11g carbohydrates, 22g fat, 3g fiber, 0mg cholesterol, 650mg sodium, 400mg potassium.

# Smoky Paprika Stock

## INGREDIENTS

- 6 cups water
- 2 onions, quartered
- 3 celery stalks, chopped
- 2 carrots, chopped
- 4 garlic cloves, crushed
- 1 bay leaf
- 2 tbsp smoked paprika
- 1 tsp olive oil
- 1 tsp sea salt (or to taste)
- 1/2 tsp black pepper

Prep Time: 10 min

Cook Time: 40 minutes

Serves: 4

## DIRECTIONS

Turn the Instant Pot on "Sauté" mode and add the olive oil. Once hot, add the onions, celery, carrots, and garlic. Sauté for about 5 minutes or until the vegetables start to soften. Sprinkle in the smoked paprika, stirring to coat the vegetables. Pour in the water, add the bay leaf, salt, and pepper. Lock the Instant Pot lid in place, set the valve to the sealing position, and select the "Soup/Broth" setting for 40 minutes. After the cooking time is finished, allow for a natural pressure release, then strain the stock, discarding the solids.

## NUTRITIONAL INFORMATION

Per serving: 40 calories, 1g protein, 10g carbohydrates, 0.5g fat, 2g fiber, 0mg cholesterol, 600mg sodium, 200mg potassium.

# Golden Turmeric Elixir

## INGREDIENTS

- 4 cups unsweetened almond milk (or any plant-based milk of your choice)
- 1 tbsp freshly grated turmeric root (or 1 tsp turmeric powder)
- 1 tsp freshly grated ginger root
- 1 cinnamon stick (or 1/2 tsp ground cinnamon)
- A pinch of black pepper (to enhance turmeric absorption)
- 1 tbsp maple syrup or agave nectar (optional, for sweetness)
- 1 tsp coconut oil (optional, for enhanced absorption and a richer mouthfeel)

 Prep Time: 5 min

 Cook Time: 10 minutes

 Serves: 4

## DIRECTIONS

In the Instant Pot, combine almond milk, turmeric, ginger, cinnamon stick, black pepper, and coconut oil, if using. Lock the Instant Pot lid in place, set the valve to the sealing position, and select the "Warm" setting for 10 minutes. After the cooking time is over, release the pressure manually and remove the cinnamon stick. Stir in the maple syrup or agave nectar, if desired. Pour the elixir through a fine sieve to serve.

## NUTRITIONAL INFORMATION

Per serving: 60 calories, 1g protein, 8g carbohydrates, 3g fat, 1g fiber, 0mg cholesterol, 85mg sodium, 50mg potassium.

# Mushroom Umami Broth

## INGREDIENTS

- 6 cups water
- 500g mixed mushrooms (like shiitake, portobello, and cremini), roughly chopped
- 1 onion, quartered
- 4 cloves garlic, smashed
- 2 tbsp tamari or soy sauce (ensure gluten-free if necessary)
- 1 tbsp olive oil
- 1 tsp dried thyme
- 2 bay leaves
- Salt and black pepper to taste
- 1 tbsp nutritional yeast (optional, for added depth and flavor)

 Prep Time: 10 min

 Cook Time: 40 minutes

 Serves: 4 servings

## DIRECTIONS

Turn the Instant Pot on "Sauté" mode. Add olive oil, followed by the mushrooms, onions, and garlic. Sauté for about 5-7 minutes until the mushrooms release their moisture and it starts to evaporate. Add the tamari or soy sauce, thyme, bay leaves, and nutritional yeast if using, stirring to combine.

Pour in the water and season with salt and pepper. Lock the Instant Pot lid in place, set the valve to the sealing position, and select the "Soup/Broth" setting for 40 minutes. After the cooking time is finished, allow for a natural pressure release, then strain the broth, discarding the solids.

## NUTRITIONAL INFORMATION

Per serving: 50 calories, 3g protein, 7g carbohydrates, 1g fat, 2g fiber, 0mg cholesterol, 400mg sodium, 300mg potassium.

# Zesty Lime Broth

## INGREDIENTS

- 6 cups water
- Juice and zest of 4 limes
- 2 stalks lemongrass, bruised and roughly chopped
- 1-inch piece of ginger, thinly sliced
- 2 cloves garlic, minced
- 2 green chilies, deseeded and thinly sliced (optional for extra heat)
- Salt to taste
- A small handful of fresh cilantro, roughly chopped
- 1 tsp olive oil

Prep Time: 5 min

Cook Time: 20 minutes

Serves: 4

## DIRECTIONS

Turn the Instant Pot on "Sauté" mode. Add olive oil, followed by the ginger, garlic, and green chilies. Sauté for about 2-3 minutes until fragrant. Add water, lime juice, lime zest, lemongrass, and salt. Stir well. Lock the Instant Pot lid in place, set the valve to the sealing position, and select the "Soup/Broth" setting for 15 minutes. Once the cooking cycle is complete, allow for a quick release of pressure. Stir in the fresh cilantro and let it sit for 5 minutes before straining the broth and discarding the solids.

## NUTRITIONAL INFORMATION

Per serving: 25 calories, 0g protein, 7g carbohydrates, 1g fat, 1g fiber, 0mg cholesterol, 150mg sodium, 50mg potassium.

# Garlicky Green Base

## INGREDIENTS

- 4 cups water
- 2 cups fresh spinach, washed and roughly chopped
- 1 cup fresh kale, stems removed and roughly chopped
- 6 garlic cloves, minced
- 1 green chili, deseeded and chopped (optional for extra heat)
- 1 medium onion, chopped
- 1 tablespoon olive oil
- Salt to taste
- 1 tsp black pepper
- 1 tsp lemon zest

Prep Time: 10 min

Cook Time: 12 minutes

Serves: 4

## DIRECTIONS

Turn on the Instant Pot to "Sauté" mode. Add the olive oil, followed by the onion, garlic, and green chili. Sauté for about 3-4 minutes until onions become translucent. Add spinach, kale, water, salt, pepper, and lemon zest. Stir well to combine. Lock the Instant Pot lid in place, set the valve to the sealing position, and select the "Soup/Broth" setting for 8 minutes. Once the cooking cycle is complete, allow for a natural release of pressure. Then, using an immersion blender, blend the mixture until smooth, creating a rich green base.

## NUTRITIONAL INFORMATION

Per serving: 70 calories, 2g protein, 11g carbohydrates, 3g fat, 2g fiber, 0mg cholesterol, 200mg sodium, 300mg potassium.

# Savory Seaweed Stock

## INGREDIENTS

- 6 cups water
- 2 sheets kombu (dried kelp)
- 1/2 cup dried wakame seaweed
- 3 green onions, chopped (white and green parts separated)
- 1-inch piece ginger, sliced
- 2 garlic cloves, crushed
- 1 tablespoon soy sauce or tamari (ensure gluten-free if necessary)
- Salt to taste

Prep Time: 5 min   Cook Time: 25 minutes   Serves: 4

## DIRECTIONS

Rinse the kombu and wakame under cold water to remove any impurities or salt. Place the water, kombu, wakame, white parts of the green onions, ginger, and garlic into the Instant Pot. Lock the Instant Pot lid in place, set the valve to the sealing position, and select the "Soup/Broth" setting for 20 minutes. Once the cooking cycle is complete, quick release the pressure. Remove and discard the kombu, wakame, and other solids. Stir in the soy sauce or tamari, and adjust seasoning with salt if needed. Garnish the stock with the green parts of the green onions before serving or using in other recipes.

## NUTRITIONAL INFORMATION

Per serving: 15 calories, 1g protein, 3g carbohydrates, 0g fat, 1g fiber, 0mg cholesterol, 350mg sodium, 50mg potassium.

# Tomato Basil Reduction

## INGREDIENTS

- 4 cups ripe tomatoes, diced
- 1/2 cup fresh basil leaves, finely chopped
- 3 cloves garlic, minced
- 1 tablespoon olive oil
- 1 teaspoon balsamic vinegar
- Salt and pepper, to taste

Prep Time: 10 min   Cook Time: 15 minutes   Serves: 4

## DIRECTIONS

Turn on the Instant Pot's sauté function and add olive oil. Once heated, add the minced garlic and sauté until fragrant. Add the diced tomatoes and balsamic vinegar to the pot. Stir to combine. Lock the Instant Pot lid in place, set the valve to the sealing position, and set it on "Manual" or "Pressure Cook" for 10 minutes. Once the cooking cycle is complete, quick release the pressure. Turn on the sauté function again and let the mixture simmer until it reduces to your desired consistency. Stir in the chopped basil and season with salt and pepper to taste. Turn off the Instant Pot and transfer the reduction to a serving dish or jar.

## NUTRITIONAL INFORMATION

Per serving: 60 calories, 1.5g protein, 8g carbohydrates, 3g fat, 2g fiber, 0mg cholesterol, 10mg sodium, 290mg potassium.

# Roasted Red Pepper Puree

## INGREDIENTS

- 4 large red bell peppers, seeds and stems removed, cut into quarters
- 2 cloves garlic, minced
- 1 tablespoon olive oil
- 1/2 teaspoon smoked paprika
- Salt and pepper, to taste
- 1/2 cup vegetable broth or water

Prep Time: 10 min

Cook Time: 20 minutes

Serves: 4

## DIRECTIONS

Place the quartered red peppers in the Instant Pot, along with the garlic, olive oil, smoked paprika, and vegetable broth. Lock the Instant Pot lid in place, set the valve to the sealing position, and set it on "Manual" or "Pressure Cook" for 10 minutes. Once the cooking cycle is complete, allow the Instant Pot to release pressure naturally for 5 minutes, then quick release any remaining pressure. Using an immersion blender or transferring to a countertop blender, blend the mixture until smooth. Season with salt and pepper to taste.

## NUTRITIONAL INFORMATION

Per serving: 90 calories, 1.5g protein, 9g carbohydrates, 5g fat, 2.5g fiber, 0mg cholesterol, 80mg sodium, 250mg potassium.

Wholesome Grains & Legumes

# Perfect Pressure-Cooked Brown Rice

## INGREDIENTS

- 2 cups brown rice, rinsed and drained
- 2.5 cups water
- 1/2 teaspoon sea salt (optional)

 Prep Time: 5 min

 Cook Time: 22 minutes

 Serves: 4

## DIRECTIONS

Add the rinsed brown rice, water, and sea salt (if using) to the Instant Pot. Lock the Instant Pot lid in place, set the valve to the sealing position, and set it on "Manual" or "Pressure Cook" for 22 minutes. Once the cooking cycle is complete, allow the Instant Pot to release pressure naturally for 10 minutes, then quick release any remaining pressure. Fluff the rice with a fork and serve as desired.

## NUTRITIONAL INFORMATION

Per serving: 215 calories, 5g protein, 45g carbohydrates, 1g fat, 3g fiber, 0mg cholesterol, 10mg sodium (without salt addition), 150mg potassium.

# Instant Pot Barley Bliss

## INGREDIENTS

- 1 cup pearl barley, rinsed and drained
- 3 cups vegetable broth
- 1 small onion, finely chopped
- 2 cloves garlic, minced
- 1 cup diced carrots
- 1/2 cup diced bell peppers (any color)
- 1 tablespoon olive oil
- 1/2 teaspoon sea salt (optional)
- 1/4 teaspoon freshly ground black pepper
- 1/4 cup fresh parsley, chopped (for garnish)

 Prep Time: 10 minutes

 Cook Time: 25 minutes

 Serves: 4

## DIRECTIONS

Turn on the Instant Pot to the "Sauté" mode and add olive oil. Once hot, add onions and garlic and sauté until translucent. Add the carrots and bell peppers to the pot and sauté for another 2-3 minutes. Stir in the pearl barley, vegetable broth, salt (if using), and black pepper. Lock the Instant Pot lid in place, set the valve to the sealing position, and set it on "Manual" or "Pressure Cook" for 25 minutes. Once the cooking cycle is complete, quick release the pressure. Garnish with fresh parsley before serving.

## NUTRITIONAL INFORMATION

Per serving: 210 calories, 6g protein, 44g carbohydrates, 3g fat, 7g fiber, 0mg cholesterol, 750mg sodium (depending on broth used), 260mg potassium.

# Chickpea Chana Masala

## INGREDIENTS

- 2 cans (15 oz each) chickpeas, drained and rinsed
- 1 large onion, finely chopped
- 3 cloves garlic, minced
- 1-inch ginger, minced
- 2 cups diced tomatoes
- 2 tablespoons olive oil or coconut oil
- 2 teaspoons garam masala
- 1 teaspoon ground turmeric, cumin, chili powder
- 1/2 teaspoon ground coriander
- 2 cups water or vegetable broth

Prep Time: 15 min

Cook Time: 25 minutes

Serves: 4

## DIRECTIONS

Turn on the Instant Pot to the "Sauté" mode and add the oil. Once hot, add onions, garlic, and ginger. Sauté until the onions become translucent. Add the spices: garam masala, turmeric, cumin, chili powder, coriander, cayenne pepper (if using), and salt. Stir well for about 1-2 minutes until fragrant. Mix in the tomatoes, chickpeas, and water or vegetable broth. Stir well to combine. Close the Instant Pot lid, set the valve to the sealing position, and set on "Manual" or "Pressure Cook" for 20 minutes. Once done, quick release the pressure. Stir in the lemon juice and adjust salt if needed.

## NUTRITIONAL INFORMATION

Per serving: 320 calories, 12g protein, 45g carbohydrates, 10g fat, 12g fiber, 0mg cholesterol, 800mg sodium (based on broth and canned chickpeas), 470mg potassium.

# Lentil and Wild Rice Pilaf

## INGREDIENTS

- 3/4 cup wild rice, rinsed and drained
- 1/2 cup green or brown lentils, rinsed and drained
- 1 onion, finely chopped
- 3 cloves garlic, minced
- 2 carrots, diced
- 2 stalks celery, diced
- 2 tablespoons olive oil or coconut oil
- 2 1/2 cups vegetable broth or water
- 1 teaspoon dried thyme
- 1/2 teaspoon dried rosemary
- 1/4 cup fresh parsley, chopped (for garnish)

Prep Time: 15 min

Cook Time: 28 minutes

Serves: 4

## DIRECTIONS

Turn on the Instant Pot to the "Sauté" mode and add the oil. Once hot, add onions, garlic, carrots, and celery. Sauté until the onions are translucent, about 3 minutes. Add wild rice, lentils, thyme, rosemary, salt, and pepper. Stir well for about 1 minute, ensuring the grains and lentils are well-coated. Pour in the vegetable broth or water and stir once more, scraping any bits off the bottom.

Close the Instant Pot lid, set the valve to the sealing position, and set on "Manual" or "Pressure Cook" for 25 minutes. Once done, let it naturally release for 10 minutes, then quick release the remaining pressure.

## NUTRITIONAL INFORMATION

Per serving: 320 calories, 13g protein, 55g carbohydrates, 6g fat, 10g fiber, 0mg cholesterol, 620mg sodium (based on broth), 400mg potassium.

# Tri-color Quinoa Medley

## INGREDIENTS

- 1 cup tri-color quinoa, rinsed and drained
- 2 cups vegetable broth
- 1/2 cup cherry tomatoes, halved
- 1/2 cup black beans, rinsed and drained
- 1/2 cup corn kernels (frozen or fresh)
- 1/4 cup red onion, finely chopped
- 2 cloves garlic, minced
- 1 tablespoon olive oil
- 1/2 teaspoon cumin powder

Prep Time: 10 min

Cook Time: 15 minutes

Serves: 4

## DIRECTIONS

Turn on the Instant Pot to the "Sauté" mode and add the olive oil. Once hot, add red onion and garlic. Sauté until the onions are translucent, about 3 minutes. Add tri-color quinoa, cumin powder, salt, and pepper. Stir well for about 2 minutes, ensuring the grains are well-coated. Pour in the vegetable broth, cherry tomatoes, black beans, and corn kernels. Give a gentle stir. Close the Instant Pot lid, set the valve to the sealing position, and set on "Manual" or "Pressure Cook" for 12 minutes. Once done, quick release the pressure. Stir in the lime juice, adjust seasoning if necessary, and garnish with fresh cilantro before serving.

## NUTRITIONAL INFORMATION

Per serving: 260 calories, 9g protein, 45g carbohydrates, 6g fat, 6g fiber, 0mg cholesterol, 480mg sodium (based on broth), 380mg potassium.

# Spiced Kidney Beans

## INGREDIENTS

- 2 cups dried kidney beans, soaked overnight
- 4 cups vegetable broth or water
- 1 medium onion, finely chopped
- 3 cloves garlic, minced
- 1 can (14.5 oz) diced tomatoes
- 2 teaspoons ground cumin
- 1 teaspoon smoked paprika
- 1/2 teaspoon cayenne pepper (adjust based on heat preference)
- 2 tablespoons olive oil
- Fresh coriander/cilantro for garnish

Prep Time: 10 min

Cook Time: 35 minutes

Serves: 4

## DIRECTIONS

On the Instant Pot's "Sauté" mode, heat the olive oil. Add the chopped onion and sauté until translucent. Add in the garlic and sauté for another minute. Add in the cumin, smoked paprika, and cayenne pepper. Stir to combine and cook for 1-2 minutes, or until fragrant. Add the soaked kidney beans, diced tomatoes, and vegetable broth or water to the pot. Stir to combine. Close the Instant Pot lid, set the valve to the sealing position, and set on "Manual" or "Pressure Cook" for 30 minutes. Once done, allow for natural pressure release for about 10 minutes, then quick release any remaining pressure. Adjust salt to taste, garnish with fresh cilantro, and serve.

## NUTRITIONAL INFORMATION

Per serving: 280 calories, 14g protein, 40g carbohydrates, 7g fat, 11g fiber, 0mg cholesterol, 450mg sodium (based on broth), 700mg potassium.

# Creamy Coconut Millet

## INGREDIENTS

- 1 cup millet, rinsed and drained
- 1 can (13.5 oz) full-fat coconut milk
- 2 cups water
- 1/4 cup shredded unsweetened coconut
- 2 tablespoons maple syrup (or to taste)
- 1 teaspoon vanilla extract
- Pinch of salt

 Prep Time: 10 min

 Cook Time: 20 minutes

 Serves: 4

## DIRECTIONS

In the Instant Pot, combine the rinsed millet, coconut milk, water, shredded coconut, maple syrup, and a pinch of salt. Secure the lid and set the valve to the sealing position. Select the "Manual" or "Pressure Cook" setting and adjust the time to 10 minutes. Once the cooking cycle is complete, allow the Instant Pot to release pressure naturally for 10 minutes. Then, carefully turn the valve to the venting position for a quick release. Stir in the vanilla extract and adjust sweetness, if desired. Serve warm.

## NUTRITIONAL INFORMATION

Per serving: 320 calories, 6g protein, 50g carbohydrates, 12g fat, 4g fiber, 0mg cholesterol, 40mg sodium, 220mg potassium.

# Buckwheat Breakfast Bowl

## INGREDIENTS

- 1 cup raw buckwheat groats, rinsed and drained
- 2.5 cups almond milk (or any plant-based milk)
- 1 ripe banana, mashed
- 1 tablespoon chia seeds
- 2 tablespoons maple syrup or agave nectar
- 1/2 teaspoon cinnamon
- 1/4 teaspoon salt
- Toppings: fresh berries, nuts, seeds, or additional sweetener as desired

 Prep Time: 5 min

 Cook Time: 12 minutes

 Serves: 4

## DIRECTIONS

In the Instant Pot, combine the buckwheat groats, almond milk, mashed banana, chia seeds, maple syrup, cinnamon, and salt. Secure the lid and set the valve to the sealing position. Choose the "Manual" or "Pressure Cook" setting and adjust the time to 7 minutes. Once the cooking cycle is complete, allow the Instant Pot to release pressure naturally for 5 minutes. Then, carefully turn the valve to the venting position for a quick release. Stir well and serve in bowls, topped with your favorite fruits, nuts, seeds, or an additional drizzle of sweetener.

## NUTRITIONAL INFORMATION

Per serving: 250 calories, 7g protein, 48g carbohydrates, 3.5g fat, 6g fiber, 0mg cholesterol, 90mg sodium, 370mg potassium.

# Spanish-Style Lentils

## INGREDIENTS

- 1 cup dry brown lentils, rinsed and drained
- 2.5 cups vegetable broth
- 1 onion, finely chopped
- 3 cloves garlic, minced
- 1 red bell pepper, diced
- 1 can (14.5 oz) diced tomatoes
- 1 teaspoon smoked paprika
- 1/2 teaspoon ground cumin
- 1/2 teaspoon turmeric
- 1/4 teaspoon chili powder (optional for some heat)
- 2 tablespoons olive oil

 Prep Time: 10 min      Cook Time: 20 minutes      Serves: 4

## DIRECTIONS

On Instant Pot's sauté mode, heat olive oil and sauté onions, garlic, and red bell pepper until onions are translucent (3-4 mins). Add lentils, diced tomatoes, smoked paprika, cumin, turmeric, chili powder, and vegetable broth. Stir well. Secure lid, set to "Manual" or "Pressure Cook" for 15 mins. After cooking, natural release for 10 mins, then quick release. Season with salt and pepper, stir, and serve hot. Garnish with fresh parsley if desired.

## NUTRITIONAL INFORMATION

Per serving: 250 calories, 13g protein, 35g carbohydrates, 7g fat, 14g fiber, 0mg cholesterol, 420mg sodium, 650mg potassium.

# Moroccan Chickpea Stew

## INGREDIENTS

- 2 cans (15 oz each) chickpeas, rinsed and drained
- 1 large onion, chopped
- 3 cloves garlic, minced
- 2 carrots, diced
- 1 red bell pepper, diced
- 2 cups diced tomatoes (canned or fresh)
- 3 cups vegetable broth
- 2 teaspoons ground cumin
- 1 teaspoon ground turmeric, cinnamon
- 1/2 teaspoon paprika
- 1/4 teaspoon cayenne pepper
- 1 bay leaf

 Prep Time: 15 min      Cook Time: 25 minutes      Serves: 4

## DIRECTIONS

Using the Instant Pot's sauté function, heat the olive oil. Add the onions, garlic, carrots, and bell pepper. Sauté for 4-5 minutes or until softened. Add the chickpeas, tomatoes, vegetable broth, cumin, turmeric, cinnamon, paprika, cayenne, and bay leaf. Mix thoroughly. Secure the lid and set the valve to the sealing position. Choose the "Manual" or "Pressure Cook" setting and adjust the time to 20 minutes. After the cooking cycle finishes, allow the Instant Pot to release pressure naturally for 10 minutes, then quick release the remaining pressure. Discard the bay leaf, season with salt and pepper, and serve hot, garnished with fresh cilantro or parsley.

## NUTRITIONAL INFORMATION

Per serving: 320 calories, 12g protein, 52g carbohydrates, 8g fat, 12g fiber, 0mg cholesterol, 480mg sodium, 700mg potassium.

# Bulgar Wheat Salad

## INGREDIENTS

- 1 cup bulgur wheat
- 2 cups water
- 1 cucumber, diced
- 1 cup cherry tomatoes, halved
- 1/4 cup red onion, finely chopped
- 1/4 cup fresh parsley, chopped
- 1/4 cup fresh mint, chopped
- 2 tablespoons olive oil
- 2 tablespoons lemon juice
- Optional: 1/4 cup Kalamata olives, pitted and chopped

 Prep Time: 15 min

 Cook Time: 12 minutes

 Serves: 4

## DIRECTIONS

In the Instant Pot, combine bulgur wheat and water. Set to "Manual" or "Pressure Cook" for 10 minutes. After cooking, let it natural release for 5 minutes, then quick release. Transfer cooked bulgur to a large bowl and let it cool. Add cucumber, cherry tomatoes, red onion, parsley, mint, and olives. Drizzle with olive oil and lemon juice, toss to combine. Season with salt and pepper before serving.

## NUTRITIONAL INFORMATION

Per serving: 210 calories, 6g protein, 36g carbohydrates, 7g fat, 8g fiber, 0mg cholesterol, 50mg sodium, 320mg potassium.

# Sweet Corn and Bean Fiesta

## INGREDIENTS

- 2 cups fresh or frozen sweet corn kernels
- 1 can (15 oz.) black beans, drained and rinsed
- 1 red bell pepper, diced
- 1/2 cup red onion, finely chopped
- 2 cloves garlic, minced
- 1 jalapeño, seeds removed and finely chopped (optional for added heat)
- 1 cup cherry tomatoes, halved
- 1 teaspoon ground cumin
- 1/2 teaspoon smoked paprika

  Prep Time: 15 min

 Cook Time: 8 minutes

 Serves: 4

## DIRECTIONS

Set the Instant Pot to "Sauté" mode. Once hot, add olive oil, onion, garlic, and jalapeño (if using). Sauté for 2-3 minutes until the onions are translucent. Add the sweet corn, black beans, red bell pepper, ground cumin, smoked paprika, salt, and pepper. Stir well to combine. Secure the lid and set the valve to the sealing position. Choose the "Manual" or "Pressure Cook" setting and adjust the time to 5 minutes. Once the cooking cycle is complete, quick release the pressure. Open the lid and stir in the cherry tomatoes, cilantro, and lime juice. Adjust the seasoning if needed and serve warm.

## NUTRITIONAL INFORMATION

Per serving: 280 calories, 11g protein, 48g carbohydrates, 7g fat, 11g fiber, 0mg cholesterol, 210mg sodium, 650mg potassium.

# Smoky Black-eyed Peas

## INGREDIENTS

- 1 cup dried black-eyed peas, soaked overnight and drained
- 1 medium onion, finely chopped
- 2 cloves garlic, minced
- 1 green bell pepper, diced
- 2 tomatoes, diced
- 1 teaspoon smoked paprika
- 1/2 teaspoon ground cumin
- 1/4 teaspoon cayenne pepper (adjust according to heat preference)
- 3 cups vegetable broth or water
- 2 tablespoons fresh cilantro, chopped

 Prep Time: 10 minutes

 Cook Time: 25 minutes

 Serves: 4

## DIRECTIONS

Set the Instant Pot to "Sauté" mode. Add olive oil, followed by onion, garlic, and bell pepper. Sauté for about 3 minutes until the onions are translucent. Add the soaked black-eyed peas, tomatoes, smoked paprika, ground cumin, cayenne pepper, and vegetable broth or water. Mix well. Secure the lid, set the valve to the sealing position, and select "Pressure Cook" or "Manual" for 20 minutes. Once the cooking cycle is complete, allow the Instant Pot to naturally release pressure for 10 minutes, then quick release the remaining pressure. Season with salt and pepper to taste, garnish with fresh cilantro, and serve warm.

## NUTRITIONAL INFORMATION

Per serving: 240 calories, 13g protein, 40g carbohydrates, 5g fat, 8g fiber, 0mg cholesterol, 280mg sodium, 650mg potassium.

# Green Lentil Curry

## INGREDIENTS

- 1 cup green lentils, rinsed and drained
- 1 medium onion, chopped
- 2 cloves garlic, minced
- 1-inch piece of ginger, minced
- 1 can (14 oz) coconut milk
- 2 cups vegetable broth
- 2 teaspoons curry powder
- 1/2 teaspoon ground turmeric
- 1/2 teaspoon ground cumin
- 1/4 teaspoon cayenne pepper (adjust according to heat preference)
- 1/2 cup diced tomatoes, chopped spinach or kale

 Prep Time: 15 min

 Cook Time: 20 minutes

 Serves: 4

## DIRECTIONS

Set the Instant Pot to "Sauté" mode. Add the oil, followed by the onion, garlic, and ginger. Sauté until the onions are translucent, about 3-4 minutes. Add the green lentils, coconut milk, vegetable broth, curry powder, turmeric, cumin, and cayenne pepper to the pot. Stir to combine. Secure the lid, set the valve to the sealing position, and select "Pressure Cook" or "Manual" for 15 minutes. Once the cooking cycle is complete, allow a natural pressure release for 10 minutes, then quick release any remaining pressure. Stir in the diced tomatoes and spinach or kale, allowing the heat from the curry to wilt the greens. Season with salt to taste and garnish with fresh cilantro leaves before serving.

## NUTRITIONAL INFORMATION

Per serving: 365 calories, 18g protein, 40g carbohydrates, 17g fat, 16g fiber, 0mg cholesterol, 320mg sodium, 720mg potassium.

# Harvest Farro Bowl

## INGREDIENTS

- 1 cup farro, rinsed and drained
- 2.5 cups vegetable broth
- 1 tablespoon olive oil
- 1 medium red onion, sliced
- 2 cloves garlic, minced
- 1 cup butternut squash, cubed
- 1/2 cup chopped kale
- 1/2 cup canned chickpeas, drained and rinsed
- 1/4 cup dried cranberries
- 1/4 cup chopped walnuts or pecans
- 1/4 teaspoon ground cinnamon
- Salt and black pepper to taste
- Fresh parsley or cilantro for garnish

Prep Time: 10 min

Cook Time: 25 minutes

Serves: 4

## DIRECTIONS

Set the Instant Pot to "Sauté" mode. Add the olive oil, followed by the red onion and garlic. Sauté until the onions are translucent, about 2-3 minutes. Add the farro, butternut squash, and vegetable broth to the pot. Stir to combine. Secure the lid, set the valve to the sealing position, and select "Pressure Cook" or "Manual" for 20 minutes. Once the cooking cycle is complete, allow a natural pressure release for 5 minutes, then quick release any remaining pressure. Stir in the chopped kale, chickpeas, dried cranberries, nuts, and cinnamon. Allow the residual heat to wilt the kale. Season with salt and black pepper to taste and garnish with fresh herbs before serving.

## NUTRITIONAL INFORMATION

Per serving: 320 calories, 10g protein, 55g carbohydrates, 8g fat, 8g fiber, 0mg cholesterol, 400mg sodium, 520mg potassium.

Satisfying
Soups &
Stews

# Tuscan White Bean Soup

## INGREDIENTS

- 2 tablespoons olive oil
- 1 large onion, chopped
- 3 cloves garlic, minced
- 2 carrots, diced
- 2 celery stalks, diced
- 1 teaspoon dried thyme
- 1 teaspoon dried rosemary
- 4 cups vegetable broth
- 2 cans (15 oz each) white beans (cannellini or navy), drained and rinsed
- 1 can (14.5 oz) diced tomatoes
- 2 cups kale or spinach, chopped
- 1 bay leaf
- Juice of half a lemon

Prep Time: 15 min

Cook Time: 30 minutes

Serves: 4

## DIRECTIONS

Set the Instant Pot to "Sauté" mode. Add olive oil, then sauté onion, garlic, carrots, and celery until soft, about 5 minutes. Add dried thyme, rosemary, beans, diced tomatoes, vegetable broth, bay leaf, salt, and black pepper. Stir to combine. Secure the lid, set the valve to sealing position, and select "Pressure Cook" or "Manual" for 20 minutes. After cooking, allow a natural release for 10 minutes before doing a quick release. Stir in the kale or spinach and lemon juice, allowing the greens to wilt from the residual heat. Adjust seasonings if necessary and garnish with fresh parsley before serving.

## NUTRITIONAL INFORMATION

Per serving: 300 calories, 14g protein, 45g carbohydrates, 7g fat, 11g fiber, 0mg cholesterol, 500mg sodium, 600mg potassium.

# Spinach and Lentil Soup

## INGREDIENTS

- 1 tablespoon olive oil
- 1 medium onion, diced
- 2 cloves garlic, minced
- 1 cup dried green lentils, rinsed and drained
- 1 large carrot, diced
- 1 celery stalk, diced
- 5 cups vegetable broth
- 1 teaspoon ground cumin
- 1/2 teaspoon ground turmeric
- 1 bay leaf
- Salt and black pepper to taste
- 3 cups fresh spinach, roughly chopped
- Juice of 1 lemon

Prep Time: 15 min

Cook Time: 25 minutes

Serves: 4

## DIRECTIONS

Set the Instant Pot to the "Sauté" function. Add olive oil, then sauté onion, garlic, carrot, and celery until the onion becomes translucent, about 4 minutes.

Add lentils, vegetable broth, cumin, turmeric, bay leaf, salt, and pepper. Mix well. Close the Instant Pot lid, set the valve to the sealing position, and cook on "Pressure Cook" or "Manual" setting for 20 minutes. Once done, let the pressure release naturally for 10 minutes, then quick release the remaining pressure. Remove the bay leaf, stir in the spinach, and let it wilt from the heat. Finish with a squeeze of lemon juice before serving.

## NUTRITIONAL INFORMATION

Per serving: 260 calories, 15g protein, 40g carbohydrates, 4g fat, 16g fiber, 0mg cholesterol, 450mg sodium, 800mg potassium.

# Creamy Tomato Basil Bisque

## INGREDIENTS

- 2 tablespoons olive oil
- 1 medium onion, diced
- 3 cloves garlic, minced
- 1 (28 oz) can whole tomatoes, undrained
- 2 cups vegetable broth
- 1 cup unsweetened coconut milk (or almond milk)
- 1/4 cup fresh basil, chopped
- 1 teaspoon dried oregano
- 1/4 teaspoon black pepper
- 1 tablespoon nutritional yeast (optional, for added creaminess and flavor)
- 1 tablespoon tomato paste

 Prep Time: 10 min

 Cook Time: 20 minutes

 Serves: 4

## DIRECTIONS

Set the Instant Pot to the "Sauté" function. Add olive oil, then sauté onion and garlic until onion is translucent, approximately 3 minutes. Add the whole tomatoes (with juice), vegetable broth, basil, oregano, salt, pepper, and tomato paste. Stir to combine. Secure the lid, set the valve to the sealing position, and cook on "Pressure Cook" or "Manual" for 15 minutes. After cooking, allow pressure to release naturally for 5 minutes, then perform a quick release. Use an immersion blender (or transfer to a blender) to puree the soup until smooth. Stir in coconut milk and nutritional yeast, then heat on "Sauté" until warmed through.

## NUTRITIONAL INFORMATION

Per serving: 220 calories, 5g protein, 25g carbohydrates, 12g fat, 6g fiber, 0mg cholesterol, 600mg sodium, 500mg potassium.

# Butternut Squash Stew

## INGREDIENTS

- 2 tablespoons olive oil
- 1 medium onion, diced
- 3 cloves garlic, minced
- 4 cups butternut squash, peeled and diced
- 2 medium carrots, sliced
- 1 red bell pepper, diced
- 2 cups vegetable broth
- 1 can (15 oz) diced tomatoes, undrained
- 1 can (15 oz) chickpeas, drained and rinsed
- 1 teaspoon ground cumin, thyme
- 1/2 teaspoon smoked paprika
- 2 cups baby spinach or kale, roughly chopped

 Prep Time: 15 min

 Cook Time: 25 minutes

 Serves: 4

## DIRECTIONS

Set the Instant Pot to the "Sauté" function. Add olive oil, followed by onion and garlic. Sauté until the onions are translucent, about 3 minutes. Add the butternut squash, carrots, bell pepper, broth, diced tomatoes, chickpeas, cumin, paprika, thyme, salt, and pepper. Stir to combine. Close the Instant Pot lid, set to "Pressure Cook" or "Manual" on high for 20 minutes. Once cooking is complete, perform a quick release. Stir in the spinach or kale until wilted. Adjust seasoning as needed and garnish with fresh herbs before serving.

## NUTRITIONAL INFORMATION

Per serving: 280 calories, 8g protein, 52g carbohydrates, 7g fat, 11g fiber, 0mg cholesterol, 650mg sodium, 900mg potassium.

# Mushroom Barley Soup

## INGREDIENTS

- 2 tablespoons olive oil
- 1 medium onion, finely chopped
- 2 cloves garlic, minced
- 1 pound assorted mushrooms (like cremini, shiitake, and oyster), sliced
- 3/4 cup pearl barley, rinsed
- 6 cups vegetable broth
- 2 carrots, peeled and diced
- 2 celery stalks, diced
- 1 teaspoon dried thyme
- 1 bay leaf
- Fresh parsley, chopped for garnish

Prep Time: 15 min     Cook Time: 30 minutes     Serves: 4

## DIRECTIONS

Set the Instant Pot to "Sauté" function. Add olive oil, onion, and garlic. Sauté until onion is translucent, about 3-4 minutes. Add mushrooms and cook until they release their juices, about 5 minutes. Add the rinsed barley, vegetable broth, carrots, celery, thyme, bay leaf, salt, and pepper. Mix well. Secure the lid on the Instant Pot and set to "Pressure Cook" or "Manual" on high for 25 minutes. After cooking, allow a natural pressure release for 10 minutes, then quick release the remaining pressure. Discard the bay leaf, adjust seasonings if necessary, and garnish with chopped parsley before serving.

## NUTRITIONAL INFORMATION

Per serving: 230 calories, 8g protein, 45g carbohydrates, 5g fat, 10g fiber, 0mg cholesterol, 850mg sodium, 550mg potassium.

# African Peanut Stew

## INGREDIENTS

- 1 large onion, diced
- 3 cloves garlic, minced
- 1 inch fresh ginger, minced
- 1 large sweet potato, peeled and diced
- 1 red bell pepper, diced
- 1 can (14 oz) diced tomatoes
- 4 cups vegetable broth
- 1/3 cup creamy peanut butter
- 1/4 teaspoon cayenne pepper (or to taste)
- 2 cups kale or collard greens, chopped and stems removed
- 1 can (14 oz) chickpeas, drained and rinsed

Prep Time: 15 min     Cook Time: 20 minutes     Serves: 4

## DIRECTIONS

Set the Instant Pot to "Sauté" function. Add olive oil, onion, garlic, and ginger. Sauté until onion is translucent, about 4-5 minutes. Add sweet potato, red bell pepper, diced tomatoes, vegetable broth, peanut butter, cumin, smoked paprika, cayenne pepper, salt, and black pepper. Stir until well combined. Secure the Instant Pot lid and set to "Pressure Cook" or "Manual" on high for 15 minutes. After cooking, quick release the pressure. Stir in the kale or collard greens and chickpeas, and let them sit in the hot stew for 5 minutes until they soften. Adjust seasonings if necessary. Serve the stew garnished with fresh herbs and crushed peanuts.

## NUTRITIONAL INFORMATION

Per serving: 390 calories, 14g protein, 50g carbohydrates, 18g fat, 10g fiber, 0mg cholesterol, 950mg sodium, 780mg potassium.

# Sweet Potato and Corn Chowder

## INGREDIENTS

- 2 tablespoons olive oil
- 1 medium onion, diced
- 3 cloves garlic, minced
- 2 medium sweet potatoes, peeled and diced
- 1 red bell pepper, diced
- 3 cups fresh or frozen corn kernels
- 4 cups vegetable broth
- 1 can (14 oz) coconut milk
- 1/2 teaspoon smoked paprika
- 1/2 teaspoon dried thyme
- 2 green onions, chopped, for garnish
- Fresh cilantro or parsley, for garnish

 Prep Time: 15 min

 Cook Time: 20 minutes

 Serves: 4

## DIRECTIONS

Set the Instant Pot to the "Sauté" function. Add olive oil, onion, and garlic. Sauté until onion is translucent, about 3-4 minutes. Add sweet potatoes, bell pepper, corn kernels, vegetable broth, coconut milk, smoked paprika, dried thyme, salt, and black pepper. Mix well. Close the Instant Pot lid, set the valve to "Sealing," and adjust to "Pressure Cook" or "Manual" on high for 15 minutes.

Once done, quick release the pressure. Stir the chowder, adjust seasonings if needed, and serve garnished with green onions and fresh herbs.

## NUTRITIONAL INFORMATION

Per serving: 400 calories, 9g protein, 65g carbohydrates, 15g fat, 10g fiber, 0mg cholesterol, 900mg sodium, 750mg potassium.

# Split Pea and Vegetable Soup

## INGREDIENTS

- 1 tablespoon olive oil
- 1 medium onion, diced
- 2 cloves garlic, minced
- 2 carrots, peeled and diced
- 2 celery stalks, diced
- 1 cup green split peas, rinsed and drained
- 1 medium potato, diced
- 6 cups vegetable broth
- 1 bay leaf
- 1/2 teaspoon dried thyme
- Salt and pepper, to taste
- 1 cup chopped kale or spinach (optional)
- Fresh parsley, for garnish

 Prep Time: 15 min

 Cook Time: 25 minutes

 Serves: 4

## DIRECTIONS

Set the Instant Pot to the "Sauté" function. Add olive oil, onion, garlic, carrots, and celery. Sauté for about 4-5 minutes or until the onions are translucent. Add the split peas, potato, vegetable broth, bay leaf, dried thyme, salt, and pepper. Stir well. Close the Instant Pot lid, set the valve to "Sealing," and adjust to "Pressure Cook" or "Manual" on high for 20 minutes. Once done, allow a natural release for 10 minutes, then perform a quick release. If desired, stir in kale or spinach until wilted. Serve hot, garnished with fresh parsley.

## NUTRITIONAL INFORMATION

Per serving: 300 calories, 18g protein, 55g carbohydrates, 3g fat, 16g fiber, 0mg cholesterol, 650mg sodium, 900mg potassium.

# Roasted Red Pepper and Tomato Soup

## INGREDIENTS

- 2 tablespoons olive oil
- 1 medium onion, diced
- 3 cloves garlic, minced
- 4 large ripe tomatoes, diced
- 2 roasted red peppers, diced (store-bought or homemade)
- 4 cups vegetable broth
- 1 teaspoon dried basil
- 1/2 teaspoon dried oregano
- Salt and pepper, to taste
- 1/2 cup unsweetened coconut milk or almond milk
- Fresh basil, for garnish

Prep Time: 10 min    Cook Time: 20 minutes    Serves: 4

## DIRECTIONS

Set the Instant Pot to the "Sauté" function. Add olive oil, onion, and garlic. Sauté for about 3-4 minutes or until the onions are translucent. Add the tomatoes, roasted red peppers, vegetable broth, dried basil, dried oregano, salt, and pepper. Stir to combine. Close the Instant Pot lid, set the valve to "Sealing," and adjust to "Pressure Cook" or "Manual" on high for 15 minutes. Once done, allow a natural release for 10 minutes, then perform a quick release. Blend the soup using an immersion blender or in batches in a traditional blender. Return to the pot, stir in the milk, and heat through on the "Sauté" function. Serve hot, garnished with fresh basil.

## NUTRITIONAL INFORMATION

Per serving: 180 calories, 4g protein, 25g carbohydrates, 8g fat, 5g fiber, 0mg cholesterol, 600mg sodium, 600mg potassium.

# Coconut Curry Lentil Stew

## INGREDIENTS

- 2 tablespoons coconut oil
- 1 large onion, diced
- 3 cloves garlic, minced
- 1 tablespoon fresh ginger, minced
- 2 tablespoons curry powder
- 1 teaspoon turmeric
- 1 cup green lentils, rinsed and drained
- 4 cups vegetable broth
- 1 can (14 oz.) full-fat coconut milk
- 1 medium carrot, diced
- 1 red bell pepper, diced
- 2 cups spinach leaves, roughly chopped

Prep Time: 15 min    Cook Time: 25 minutes    Serves: 4

## DIRECTIONS

Set the Instant Pot to the "Sauté" mode. Melt the coconut oil, then add onions, garlic, and ginger. Sauté until the onions are translucent, about 4 minutes. Add the curry powder and turmeric, stirring well to coat the onion mixture. Cook for another 1 minute until fragrant. Mix in lentils, vegetable broth, coconut milk, carrot, and bell pepper. Stir well to combine. Close the Instant Pot lid, set the valve to "Sealing", and adjust to "Pressure Cook" or "Manual" on high for 20 minutes. Allow a natural release for 10 minutes, then perform a quick release. Stir in the spinach leaves until wilted, season with salt and pepper to taste, and serve hot with fresh cilantro and a squeeze of lime.

## NUTRITIONAL INFORMATION

Per serving: 480 calories, 18g protein, 45g carbohydrates, 28g fat, 15g fiber, 0mg cholesterol, 700mg sodium, 800mg potassium.

# Creamy Broccoli Almond Soup

## INGREDIENTS

- 2 tablespoons olive oil
- 1 large onion, chopped
- 3 cloves garlic, minced
- 4 cups broccoli florets
- 1/2 cup raw almonds, soaked overnight and drained
- 4 cups vegetable broth
- 1 cup unsweetened almond milk
- 1 tablespoon nutritional yeast (optional, for cheesy flavor)
- 2 teaspoons lemon juice
- Almond slices and fresh herbs, for garnish

 Prep Time: 15 min

 Cook Time: 20 minutes

 Serves: 4

## DIRECTIONS

In Instant Pot's "Sauté" mode, heat olive oil and sauté onions and garlic until translucent (about 3 mins). Add broccoli, soaked almonds, and vegetable broth; stir. Close the lid, set to "Pressure Cook" or "Manual" on high for 15 mins. Allow natural release for 10 mins, then quick release. Puree the soup until smooth with an immersion blender or in batches in a regular blender. Return to the pot, stir in almond milk, salt, pepper, nutritional yeast, and lemon juice. Heat for 2-3 mins on "Sauté" mode. Serve hot, garnished with almond slices and fresh herbs.

## NUTRITIONAL INFORMATION

Per serving: 220 calories, 8g protein, 20g carbohydrates, 14g fat, 7g fiber, 0mg cholesterol, 600mg sodium, 650mg potassium.

# Minestrone Delight

## INGREDIENTS

- 1 medium onion, diced
- 2 cloves garlic, minced
- 2 carrots, sliced
- 2 celery stalks, chopped
- 1 zucchini, diced
- 1 cup green beans, chopped
- 1 red bell pepper, diced
- 4 cups vegetable broth
- 1 can (15 oz.) diced tomatoes, undrained
- 1/2 cup pasta (e.g. elbow or ditalini)
- 1 can (15 oz.) kidney beans, drained and rinsed
- 1 teaspoon dried basil, oregano
- 2 cups spinach or kale, roughly chopped

 Prep Time: 20 min

 Cook Time: 25 minutes

 Serves: 4

## DIRECTIONS

Set the Instant Pot to "Sauté" mode. Add olive oil, then stir in onion, garlic, carrots, and celery. Sauté until onions are translucent, about 4 minutes. Add zucchini, green beans, bell pepper, vegetable broth, diced tomatoes, pasta, kidney beans, basil, oregano, salt, and pepper to the pot. Stir well. Secure the Instant Pot lid, set the valve to "Sealing", and adjust to "Pressure Cook" or "Manual" on high for 7 minutes. After cooking, allow a natural release for 10 minutes, then perform a quick release. Open the lid, set the Instant Pot back to "Sauté" mode. Stir in the spinach or kale, cooking until wilted. Turn off the pot and mix in fresh parsley and lemon juice. Serve hot, optionally garnished with nutritional yeast or vegan parmesan for an extra flavor boost.

## NUTRITIONAL INFORMATION

Per serving: 280 calories, 12g protein, 48g carbohydrates, 5g fat, 13g fiber, 0mg cholesterol, 850mg sodium, 780mg potassium.

# Chickpea Lemon Spinach Stew

## INGREDIENTS

- 2 tablespoons olive oil
- 1 medium onion, diced
- 3 cloves garlic, minced
- 1 can (15 oz.) chickpeas, drained and rinsed
- 4 cups vegetable broth
- 1 can (14.5 oz.) diced tomatoes, undrained
- 1 teaspoon ground cumin
- 1/2 teaspoon turmeric
- 1/2 teaspoon smoked paprika
- 3 cups fresh spinach, roughly chopped
- Fresh parsley, for garnish

 Prep Time: 15 min

 Cook Time: 20 minutes

 Serves: 4

## DIRECTIONS

In "Sauté" mode, add olive oil, onion, and garlic to the Instant Pot. Sauté until onions are translucent (3-4 mins). Add chickpeas, vegetable broth, diced tomatoes, lemon zest, lemon juice, cumin, turmeric, smoked paprika, salt, and black pepper. Stir well. Secure the lid, set to "Pressure Cook" or "Manual" on high for 10 mins. After cooking, natural release for 10 mins, then quick release. Open the lid, stir in chopped spinach; let it wilt from residual heat. Stand for a couple of minutes. Serve hot, garnished with fresh parsley.

## NUTRITIONAL INFORMATION

Per serving: 240 calories, 10g protein, 35g carbohydrates, 7g fat, 8g fiber, 0mg cholesterol, 800mg sodium, 550mg potassium.

# Thai Ginger Soup

## INGREDIENTS

- 4 cloves garlic, minced
- 2 inches fresh ginger, grated
- 1 medium onion, diced
- 2 medium carrots, sliced into thin rounds
- 1 bell pepper, sliced
- 4 cups vegetable broth
- 1 can (13.5 oz.) full-fat coconut milk
- 2 tablespoons soy sauce or tamari
- 1 teaspoon brown sugar or coconut sugar
- 1/2 cup sliced mushrooms, cubed tofu
- 1 red chili, sliced

 Prep Time: 15 min

 Cook Time: 15 minutes

 Serves: 4

## DIRECTIONS

Set the Instant Pot to the "Sauté" mode. Add coconut oil, followed by garlic, ginger, and onion. Sauté until onions are translucent, about 3-4 minutes. Add carrots, bell pepper, vegetable broth, coconut milk, soy sauce, lime juice, sugar, mushrooms, and tofu. Stir well to combine. Secure the Instant Pot lid, set the valve to "Sealing", and adjust to "Pressure Cook" or "Manual" on high for 8 minutes. Once completed, allow a natural release for 5 minutes, then perform a quick release. Taste and adjust seasoning with salt, pepper, and more lime juice if desired. Serve hot, garnished with fresh cilantro, green onions, and sliced chili for those who like it spicy.

## NUTRITIONAL INFORMATION

Per serving: 280 calories, 7g protein, 20g carbohydrates, 20g fat, 4g fiber, 0mg cholesterol, 950mg sodium, 500mg potassium.

# Instant Pot Vegetable Gumbo

## INGREDIENTS

- 2 tablespoons olive oil
- 1 large onion, chopped
- 3 celery stalks, chopped
- 1 bell pepper, chopped
- 4 cloves garlic, minced
- 1/4 cup all-purpose flour
- 4 cups vegetable broth
- 1 can (14 oz.) diced tomatoes
- 2 cups sliced okra (fresh or frozen)
- 1 zucchini, diced
- 2 teaspoons Cajun or Creole seasoning
- 1 teaspoon smoked paprika
- 1/2 teaspoon dried thyme
- 2 bay leaves
- 1 cup corn kernels (fresh or frozen)
- Salt and pepper, to taste
- 2 green onions, sliced, for garnish
- Fresh parsley, for garnish

Prep Time: 20 min

Cook Time: 25 minutes

Serves: 4

## DIRECTIONS

Turn on the Instant Pot's "Sauté" mode. Add the olive oil, onion, celery, and bell pepper. Sauté until the vegetables are softened, about 5 minutes. Add garlic and cook for an additional minute. Sprinkle the flour over the vegetables and stir to coat, cooking for 2-3 minutes to form a roux. Pour in the vegetable broth slowly, stirring constantly to avoid lumps. Add the diced tomatoes, okra, zucchini, Cajun seasoning, smoked paprika, thyme, and bay leaves. Mix well.

Secure the Instant Pot lid, set the valve to "Sealing", and adjust to "Pressure Cook" or "Manual" on high for 15 minutes. Once the cooking is done, perform a quick release. Stir in corn kernels and adjust seasoning with salt and pepper. Serve hot, garnished with sliced green onions and fresh parsley.

## NUTRITIONAL INFORMATION

Per serving: 190 calories, 6g protein, 36g carbohydrates, 5g fat, 6g fiber, 0mg cholesterol, 800mg sodium, 600mg potassium.

# Satisfying Soups & Stews

# Creamy Mushroom Risotto

## INGREDIENTS

- 1 tablespoon olive oil
- 1 small onion, finely chopped
- 3 garlic cloves, minced
- 2 cups Arborio rice
- 4 cups sliced mushrooms (button or cremini)
- 4-5 cups vegetable broth (low sodium)
- 1 cup unsweetened almond milk
- 1/4 cup nutritional yeast (or more to taste)
- Fresh parsley, chopped (for garnish)
- Lemon zest (optional, for garnish)

Prep Time: 15 min

Cook Time: 20 minutes

Serves: 4

## DIRECTIONS

Turn on the Instant Pot's "Sauté" mode. Add the olive oil followed by the onions and garlic. Sauté until the onions become translucent. Add the Arborio rice and sliced mushrooms, stirring for about 2 minutes until the mushrooms begin to release their juices. Pour in 4 cups of vegetable broth and mix well. Ensure that the rice is submerged. Secure the Instant Pot lid, set the valve to "Sealing", and adjust to "Pressure Cook" or "Manual" on high for 6 minutes. Once done, perform a quick release. Stir in the almond milk and nutritional yeast, adding extra broth if needed for desired consistency. Season with salt and pepper. Serve warm, garnished with fresh parsley and optional lemon zest.

## NUTRITIONAL INFORMATION

Per serving: 350 calories, 10g protein, 70g carbohydrates, 4g fat, 4g fiber, 0mg cholesterol, 200mg sodium, 300mg potassium.

# Spinach and Artichoke Penne

## INGREDIENTS

- 2 cups penne pasta (whole grain or gluten-free, if preferred)
- 2 cups vegetable broth
- 1 tablespoon olive oil
- 3 garlic cloves, minced
- 1 medium onion, finely chopped
- 1 can (14 oz.) artichoke hearts, drained and chopped
- 3 cups fresh spinach, roughly chopped
- 1/4 cup unsweetened almond milk
- 1/4 cup nutritional yeast
- 1/2 teaspoon red pepper flakes (optional)

Prep Time: 10 min

Cook Time: 8 minutes

Serves: 4

## DIRECTIONS

Turn on the Instant Pot's "Sauté" mode. Add olive oil followed by garlic and onion. Sauté until onion becomes translucent. Add in the penne, vegetable broth, artichoke hearts, spinach, and red pepper flakes. Stir to combine and ensure the pasta is submerged in the broth. Secure the Instant Pot lid, set the valve to "Sealing", and adjust to "Pressure Cook" or "Manual" on high for 4 minutes. Once done, perform a quick release. Stir in almond milk, nutritional yeast, lemon zest, and juice. Adjust seasoning with salt and black pepper. Serve immediately.

## NUTRITIONAL INFORMATION

Per serving: 320 calories, 11g protein, 60g carbohydrates, 4.5g fat, 7g fiber, 0mg cholesterol, 250mg sodium, 420mg potassium.

# Zucchini and Lemon Spaghetti

## INGREDIENTS

- 2 medium zucchinis, spiralized or thinly sliced
- 8 oz spaghetti (whole grain or gluten-free, if preferred)
- 2 1/2 cups vegetable broth
- 2 tablespoons olive oil
- 4 garlic cloves, minced
- Zest and juice of 2 lemons
- 1/4 cup fresh basil, chopped
- 1/4 cup nutritional yeast (optional for a cheesy flavor)
- Fresh parsley for garnish

Prep Time: 10 minutes

Cook Time: 8 minutes

Serves: 4

## DIRECTIONS

In Instant Pot's "Sauté" mode, add olive oil and garlic. Sauté until garlic is fragrant (about 1 min). Break spaghetti in half, add to the pot with vegetable broth, ensuring it's submerged. Secure the lid, set to "Pressure Cook" or "Manual" on high for 5 mins. After cooking, perform a quick release. Stir in zucchini noodles, lemon zest, lemon juice, basil, and nutritional yeast. Toss until zucchini slightly wilts from residual heat. Season with salt, black pepper, and optional red pepper flakes. Garnish with fresh parsley before serving.

## NUTRITIONAL INFORMATION

Per serving: 310 calories, 9g protein, 54g carbohydrates, 7g fat, 4g fiber, 0mg cholesterol, 190mg sodium, 380mg potassium.

# Instant Pot Ratatouille Risotto

## INGREDIENTS

- 1 cup Arborio rice
- 2 1/2 cups vegetable broth
- 1 medium zucchini, diced
- 1 medium eggplant, diced
- 1 red bell pepper, diced
- 2 medium tomatoes, diced
- 1 large onion, diced
- 3 garlic cloves, minced
- 2 tbsp olive oil
- 1/2 tsp dried basil
- 1/2 tsp dried thyme
- 1/2 tsp dried oregano
- 1/4 cup fresh basil, chopped for garnish
- 1/4 cup nutritional yeast (optional for a cheesy flavor)

Prep Time: 15 min

Cook Time: 25 minutes

Serves: 4

## DIRECTIONS

Turn the Instant Pot on "Sauté" mode. Add olive oil, followed by onions and garlic. Sauté until translucent, about 2-3 minutes. Add the zucchini, eggplant, bell pepper, and tomatoes to the pot. Sauté for another 5 minutes until slightly softened. Stir in the Arborio rice, dried herbs, salt, and pepper. Add vegetable broth and mix well. Lock the Instant Pot lid, set the valve to "Sealing", and cook on "Pressure Cook" or "Manual" on high for 7 minutes. Once done, perform a quick release. Stir in nutritional yeast, if using. Adjust seasoning and serve hot garnished with fresh basil.

## NUTRITIONAL INFORMATION

Per serving: 320 calories, 7g protein, 58g carbohydrates, 8g fat, 5g fiber, 0mg cholesterol, 220mg sodium, 490mg potassium.

# Sun-Dried Tomato Fettuccine

## INGREDIENTS

- 8 oz fettuccine pasta
- 1 cup sun-dried tomatoes (oil-packed), drained and chopped
- 3 cloves garlic, minced
- 1 large onion, thinly sliced
- 2 1/2 cups vegetable broth
- 1/4 cup fresh basil, chopped
- 2 tbsp olive oil from the sun-dried tomatoes jar
- 1 tsp dried oregano
- 1/4 cup nutritional yeast or vegan parmesan (optional)
- 1/4 cup Kalamata olives, pitted and sliced (optional)
- Zest of 1 lemon

 Prep Time: 10 min

 Cook Time: 15 minutes

 Serves: 4

## DIRECTIONS

Turn on the Instant Pot to "Sauté" mode. Add the sun-dried tomato olive oil, garlic, and onion. Sauté for 2-3 minutes until the onion is translucent. Add the sun-dried tomatoes, dried oregano, salt, pepper, and fettuccine (broken in half). Pour in the vegetable broth, ensuring the pasta is mostly submerged. Close the lid, set the valve to "Sealing", and cook on "Pressure Cook" or "Manual" on high for 8 minutes. Once done, perform a quick release. Stir in the fresh basil, lemon zest, nutritional yeast or vegan parmesan, and Kalamata olives if using. Adjust seasoning and serve immediately.

## NUTRITIONAL INFORMATION

Per serving: 380 calories, 12g protein, 62g carbohydrates, 9g fat, 6g fiber, 0mg cholesterol, 310mg sodium, 650mg potassium.

# Butternut Squash Mac and 'Cheese'

## INGREDIENTS

- 8 oz macaroni pasta
- 2 cups butternut squash, peeled and cubed
- 2 1/2 cups vegetable broth
- 1/2 cup raw cashews (soaked for 2 hours, then drained)
- 1/4 cup nutritional yeast
- 3 cloves garlic, minced
- 1/2 cup unsweetened almond milk
- 1 tsp smoked paprika
- 1 tsp onion powder
- Optional toppings: toasted bread crumbs, chopped parsley

 Prep Time: 15 min

 Cook Time: 20 minutes

 Serves: 4

## DIRECTIONS:

In the Instant Pot, combine the macaroni, butternut squash, garlic, vegetable broth, and olive oil. Stir to ensure pasta is submerged in the broth. Close the lid, set the valve to "Sealing", and cook on "Pressure Cook" or "Manual" on high for 5 minutes. Once done, perform a quick release. Blend the soaked cashews and almond milk in a blender until smooth and creamy. Add this mixture to the Instant Pot, followed by the nutritional yeast, smoked paprika, onion powder, salt, and pepper. Stir until well combined and creamy. Adjust seasonings to taste and serve hot. Garnish with optional toppings if desired.

## NUTRITIONAL INFORMATION

Per serving: 385 calories, 13g protein, 60g carbohydrates, 10g fat, 5g fiber, 0mg cholesterol, 320mg sodium, 480mg potassium.

# Basil Pesto Pasta

## INGREDIENTS

- 8 oz whole wheat spaghetti or your choice of pasta
- 2 1/2 cups water
- 2 cups fresh basil leaves, packed
- 1/2 cup raw cashews (soaked for 2 hours, then drained)
- 3 cloves garlic, roughly chopped
- 1/4 cup nutritional yeast
- 1/2 cup extra-virgin olive oil
- Juice of 1 lemon
- Cherry tomatoes and arugula for garnish (optional)

 Prep Time: 15 min

  Cook Time: 15 minutes

 Serves: 4

## DIRECTIONS

In the Instant Pot, place the pasta and water ensuring that the pasta is submerged. Seal the Instant Pot and set it on "Manual" or "Pressure Cook" for half the time suggested on the pasta package (usually about 4-5 minutes for spaghetti). Once done, perform a quick release. While the pasta is cooking, in a blender or food processor, combine the basil, soaked cashews, garlic, nutritional yeast, olive oil, lemon juice, salt, and pepper. Blend until smooth to create the pesto. After releasing the pressure from the Instant Pot, stir in the pesto with the pasta until evenly coated. Serve immediately, garnishing with cherry tomatoes and arugula if desired.

## NUTRITIONAL INFORMATION

Per serving: 470 calories, 12g protein, 58g carbohydrates, 23g fat, 8g fiber, 0mg cholesterol, 35mg sodium, 420mg potassium.

# Wild Mushroom and Asparagus Risotto

## INGREDIENTS

- 1 cup Arborio rice
- 2 1/2 cups vegetable broth (low sodium)
- 1/2 cup dry white wine (or additional broth)
- 1 cup wild mushrooms (such as chanterelles, oyster, and shiitake), cleaned and sliced
- 1 bunch asparagus, trimmed and cut into 1-inch pieces
- 1 small onion, finely chopped
- 3 cloves garlic, minced
- 1/4 cup nutritional yeast (for a cheesy flavor)
- Fresh parsley, chopped (for garnish)

 Prep Time: 15 min

 Cook Time: 25 minutes

 Serves: 4

## DIRECTIONS

Turn on the Instant Pot to 'Sauté' mode. Add olive oil, followed by onions and garlic. Sauté until onions are translucent. Add the wild mushrooms and asparagus pieces to the pot and sauté for another 3-4 minutes until slightly softened. Add Arborio rice to the pot, stirring for 1-2 minutes to toast it lightly. Pour in the white wine, stirring until most of it is absorbed. Pour in the vegetable broth, season with salt and pepper, then seal the Instant Pot. Set it on "Manual" or "Pressure Cook" for 6 minutes. Once done, perform a quick release. Stir in nutritional yeast for a cheesy flavor, adjust seasoning if needed. Garnish with fresh parsley before serving.

## NUTRITIONAL INFORMATION

Per serving: 340 calories, 9g protein, 59g carbohydrates, 6g fat, 4g fiber, 0mg cholesterol, 120mg sodium, 420mg potassium.

# Lemon Herb Orzo Salad

## INGREDIENTS

- 1 cup orzo pasta (whole wheat for added fiber, if preferred)
- 2 cups vegetable broth (low sodium)
- 1 cup cherry tomatoes, halved
- 1 cucumber, diced
- 1/4 cup fresh parsley, chopped
- 1/4 cup fresh mint, chopped
- Zest and juice of 1 lemon
- 2 cloves garlic, minced
- 1/4 cup Kalamata olives, pitted and chopped
- 2 tablespoons capers, drained

 Prep Time: 10 minutes

 Cook Time: 6 minutes

 Serves: 4

## DIRECTIONS

In the Instant Pot, add the orzo and vegetable broth. Set it to "Manual" or "Pressure Cook" for 4 minutes. Once done, quick release the pressure and drain any excess liquid. Transfer the cooked orzo to a large bowl, letting it cool for a few minutes. In a separate bowl, whisk together olive oil, lemon zest, lemon juice, garlic, salt, and pepper to make the dressing. Add cherry tomatoes, cucumber, parsley, mint, olives, and capers to the orzo. Pour the dressing over and toss to combine. Chill in the refrigerator for at least an hour before serving. Adjust seasonings if necessary.

## NUTRITIONAL INFORMATION

Per serving: 280 calories, 8g protein, 42g carbohydrates, 8g fat, 4g fiber, 0mg cholesterol, 220mg sodium, 320mg potassium.

# Garlic and Olive Spaghetti

## INGREDIENTS

- 8 oz whole wheat spaghetti
- 2 cups vegetable broth (low sodium)
- 1/4 cup extra-virgin olive oil
- 6-8 cloves garlic, finely sliced
- 1/2 cup Kalamata olives, pitted and chopped
- 1/4 teaspoon red pepper flakes (optional for a bit of heat)
- Salt and black pepper, to taste
- 1/4 cup fresh parsley, chopped
- Zest of 1 lemon

 Prep Time: 10 min

 Cook Time: 8 minutes

 Serves: 4

## DIRECTIONS

Break the spaghetti in half and place them in the Instant Pot. Add the vegetable broth, ensuring the spaghetti is mostly submerged. Set the Instant Pot to "Manual" or "Pressure Cook" for 4 minutes. Once done, quick release the pressure and drain any excess liquid if necessary. Using the "Sauté" function, heat the olive oil. Add the sliced garlic and red pepper flakes (if using). Sauté until garlic is golden, being careful not to burn it. Add the cooked spaghetti back into the Instant Pot. Toss in the olives, lemon zest, parsley, salt, and black pepper. Stir until well combined and heated through. Serve immediately, garnished with additional parsley or lemon zest if desired.

## NUTRITIONAL INFORMATION

Per serving: 360 calories, 10g protein, 56g carbohydrates, 12g fat, 8g fiber, 0mg cholesterol, 250mg sodium, 320mg potassium.

# Spinach Walnut Pasta

## INGREDIENTS

- 8 oz whole wheat penne pasta
- 2 cups fresh spinach, roughly chopped
- 1/2 cup walnuts, toasted and coarsely chopped
- 3 cloves garlic, minced
- 1/4 cup extra-virgin olive oil
- 1/2 teaspoon red pepper flakes (optional)
- 2 cups vegetable broth (low sodium)
- Juice and zest of 1 lemon
- Salt and black pepper, to taste
- Fresh basil leaves for garnish (optional)

Prep Time: 10 min

Cook Time: 8 minutes

Serves: 4

## DIRECTIONS

Add pasta and vegetable broth to the Instant Pot, ensuring the pasta is submerged in the broth. Set the Instant Pot to "Manual" or "Pressure Cook" for 4 minutes. Once cooking is completed, quick release the pressure. If there's excess liquid, drain the pasta. Using the "Sauté" function, heat the olive oil. Add garlic and red pepper flakes (if using). Sauté until garlic turns fragrant. Add the spinach and cook until just wilted. Mix in the walnuts, lemon juice, lemon zest, and season with salt and pepper. Add the cooked pasta back into the Instant Pot, tossing to combine everything well. Garnish with fresh basil leaves before serving.

## NUTRITIONAL INFORMATION

Per serving: 420 calories, 12g protein, 58g carbohydrates, 18g fat, 9g fiber, 0mg cholesterol, 250mg sodium, 320mg potassium.

# Tomato Capers Rotini

## INGREDIENTS

- 8 oz rotini pasta (whole wheat for added nutrition)
- 1 can (15 oz) diced tomatoes, with juice
- 2 tablespoons capers, drained and rinsed
- 3 cloves garlic, minced
- 1 small red onion, thinly sliced
- 2 cups vegetable broth (low sodium)
- 1/2 teaspoon dried oregano
- 1/2 teaspoon dried basil
- 1/4 cup fresh parsley, chopped (for garnish)
- Red pepper flakes (optional for added heat)

Prep Time: 15 minutes

Cook Time: 7 minutes

Serves: 4

## DIRECTIONS

Add rotini, diced tomatoes with juice, garlic, red onion, capers, vegetable broth, oregano, basil, and a pinch of salt and black pepper to the Instant Pot. Ensure the pasta is submerged in the liquid. Seal the Instant Pot and set it to "Manual" or "Pressure Cook" for 5 minutes. Once the cooking is completed, quick release the pressure. Stir the pasta well, adjusting salt and pepper to taste. Using the "Sauté" function, drizzle in the olive oil and add red pepper flakes if using. Stir for 1-2 minutes until well combined. Serve the pasta in bowls and garnish with fresh parsley.

## NUTRITIONAL INFORMATION

Per serving: 370 calories, 11g protein, 70g carbohydrates, 7g fat, 8g fiber, 0mg cholesterol, 300mg sodium, 410mg potassium.

# Bell Pepper Risotto

## INGREDIENTS

- 1 cup Arborio rice
- 2 cups vegetable broth (low sodium)
- 1 red bell pepper, finely chopped
- 1 yellow bell pepper, finely chopped
- 1 green bell pepper, finely chopped
- 1 onion, finely chopped
- 3 cloves garlic, minced
- 1/4 cup nutritional yeast
- 1 tablespoon fresh parsley, chopped (for garnish)
- 1/4 cup white wine (optional)
- 1 teaspoon lemon zest

 Prep Time: 15 min

Cook Time: 20 minutes

 Serves: 4

## DIRECTIONS

Turn on the Instant Pot and set it to the "Sauté" function. Add olive oil, onion, and garlic. Sauté until translucent. Add the Arborio rice and stir, letting it toast slightly. If using, pour in the white wine and let it evaporate. Add the chopped bell peppers and mix well. Pour in the vegetable broth, ensuring the rice is submerged. Season with salt and pepper. Close the lid, set the Instant Pot to "Manual" or "Pressure Cook" mode, and adjust the time to 7 minutes. Once done, quick release the pressure. Stir in the nutritional yeast or vegan parmesan and lemon zest until creamy. Garnish with fresh parsley before serving.

## NUTRITIONAL INFORMATION

Per serving: 330 calories, 7g protein, 58g carbohydrates, 7g fat, 3g fiber, 0mg cholesterol, 250mg sodium, 320mg potassium.

# Eggplant Parmesan Pasta

## INGREDIENTS

- 2 medium-sized eggplants, diced into 1-inch cubes
- 2 cups pasta of choice
- 1 onion, finely chopped
- 3 cloves garlic, minced
- 1 can (28 oz) crushed tomatoes
- 1/4 cup fresh basil leaves, chopped
- 2 tablespoons nutritional yeast (or vegan parmesan)
- 1 teaspoon dried oregano
- 2 cups water or vegetable broth (low sodium)
- 1/4 cup vegan mozzarella shreds (optional)

 Prep Time: 20 min

 Cook Time: 15 minutes

 Serves: 4

## DIRECTIONS

In Instant Pot's "Sauté" function, heat olive oil, sauté onion and garlic until translucent. Add diced eggplant, sauté for 3-4 mins until softened. Stir in crushed tomatoes, water/vegetable broth, pasta, dried oregano, salt, and pepper. Ensure pasta is submerged. Close the lid, set to "Manual" or "Pressure Cook" for 8 mins. Quick release pressure when done. Stir in nutritional yeast or vegan parmesan and fresh basil. Optionally, top with vegan mozzarella shreds before serving.

## NUTRITIONAL INFORMATION

Per serving: 420 calories, 12g protein, 80g carbohydrates, 8g fat, 11g fiber, 0mg cholesterol, 480mg sodium, 820mg potassium.

# Sweet Corn and Basil Pasta

## INGREDIENTS

- 2 cups pasta of choice (penne or spaghetti work well)
- 3 cups fresh corn kernels (about 3-4 ears of corn)
- 2 tablespoons extra-virgin olive oil
- 1 onion, finely chopped
- 3 cloves garlic, minced
- 1/4 cup fresh basil leaves, chopped
- 1 red bell pepper, diced
- 2.5 cups vegetable broth (low sodium)
- Salt and black pepper, to taste
- 1/4 cup nutritional yeast or vegan parmesan (optional)
- Lemon zest from 1 lemon

Prep Time: 10 min

Cook Time: 12 minutes

Serves: 4

## DIRECTIONS

Activate the "Sauté" function on the Instant Pot. Add the olive oil, followed by the onion and garlic. Sauté until translucent. Add the corn and bell pepper, and sauté for another 2 minutes. Incorporate the pasta, vegetable broth, salt, and pepper. Ensure that the pasta is submerged in the liquid. Secure the lid, set the Instant Pot to "Manual" or "Pressure Cook" mode, and adjust the time to 8 minutes. Once completed, quick release the pressure. Stir in the fresh basil, nutritional yeast or vegan parmesan, and lemon zest. Mix well before serving.

## NUTRITIONAL INFORMATION

Per serving: 390 calories, 13g protein, 70g carbohydrates, 8g fat, 7g fiber, 0mg cholesterol, 320mg sodium, 460mg potassium.

Sensational
Sides

# Garlic Herb Steamed Vegetables

## INGREDIENTS

- 2 cups broccoli florets
- 2 cups cauliflower florets
- 1 cup carrot slices
- 1 cup snap peas or green beans
- 1 red bell pepper, sliced into strips
- 4 cloves garlic, minced
- 1 tablespoon extra-virgin olive oil
- 2 teaspoons mixed dried herbs (thyme, rosemary, oregano, basil)
- 1 cup water
- Salt and pepper, to taste
- Fresh parsley or dill for garnish (optional)

Prep Time: 15 minutes

Cook Time: 4 minutes

Serves: 4

## DIRECTIONS

In a bowl, toss vegetables with garlic, olive oil, mixed herbs, salt, and pepper until evenly coated. Add 1 cup of water to the Instant Pot, followed by the trivet or a steamer basket. Arrange the seasoned vegetables on the trivet or in the steamer basket. Secure the lid, set the Instant Pot to "Steam" mode, and adjust the time to 2 minutes. Once done, quick release the pressure. Serve hot and garnish with fresh parsley or dill if desired.

## NUTRITIONAL INFORMATION

Per serving: 95 calories, 4g protein, 16g carbohydrates, 3g fat, 5g fiber, 0mg cholesterol, 65mg sodium, 420mg potassium.

# Rosemary Roasted Potatoes

## INGREDIENTS

- 2 pounds baby potatoes, halved or quartered based on size
- 2 tablespoons extra-virgin olive oil
- 3 cloves garlic, minced
- 2 tablespoons fresh rosemary, finely chopped (or 1 tablespoon dried rosemary)
- Salt and pepper, to taste
- 1 cup water

Prep Time: 10 min

Cook Time: 20 minutes

Serves: 4

## DIRECTIONS

In a large bowl, toss the potatoes with olive oil, garlic, rosemary, salt, and pepper until well coated. Add the 1 cup of water to the Instant Pot, followed by a trivet. Arrange the seasoned potatoes on the trivet. Secure the lid, set the Instant Pot to "Manual" or "Pressure Cook" mode, and adjust the time to 7 minutes. Once done, quick release the pressure. Remove potatoes and spread on a baking sheet. For a crisp finish, broil the potatoes in an oven or air fryer for 5-7 minutes or until they get a golden-brown crispy layer.

## NUTRITIONAL INFORMATION

Per serving: 220 calories, 4g protein, 40g carbohydrates, 7g fat, 4g fiber, 0mg cholesterol, 10mg sodium, 950mg potassium.

# Instant Pot Stuffed Bell Peppers

## INGREDIENTS

- 4 large bell peppers (any color), tops removed and seeds cleaned out
- 1 cup cooked quinoa
- 1 can (15 oz) black beans, drained and rinsed
- 1 cup corn kernels, fresh or frozen
- 1 can (14.5 oz) diced tomatoes, drained slightly
- 1 teaspoon ground cumin
- 1 teaspoon chili powder
- Salt and pepper, to taste
- 1 cup water
- Fresh cilantro, for garnish (optional)

 Prep Time: 15 minutes

 Cook Time: 20 minutes

 Serves: 4

## DIRECTIONS

In a large mixing bowl, combine cooked quinoa, black beans, corn, diced tomatoes, cumin, chili powder, salt, and pepper. Mix thoroughly. Stuff each bell pepper with the quinoa mixture, pressing down gently to pack the filling. Pour 1 cup of water into the Instant Pot. Place the stuffed bell peppers into the pot, standing upright. Secure the lid and set the Instant Pot to "Manual" or "Pressure Cook" mode, adjusting the time to 10 minutes. Once done, let the pressure release naturally for 5 minutes, then quick release the remaining pressure.

## NUTRITIONAL INFORMATION

Per serving: 230 calories, 9g protein, 45g carbohydrates, 2g fat, 9g fiber, 0mg cholesterol, 300mg sodium, 750mg potassium.

# Cilantro Lime Cauliflower Rice

## INGREDIENTS

- 1 large head of cauliflower, cut into florets
- 1 tablespoon olive oil
- Juice and zest of 1 lime
- 1/2 cup fresh cilantro, finely chopped
- Salt and pepper, to taste
- 1/4 cup water

 Prep Time: 10 min

 Cook Time: 5 minutes

 Serves: 4

## DIRECTIONS

Place cauliflower florets into a food processor and pulse until they reach a rice-like consistency. Pour the water into the Instant Pot and then add the riced cauliflower. Drizzle olive oil over the cauliflower rice, and season with salt and pepper. Stir to combine. Secure the lid and set the Instant Pot to "Manual" or "Pressure Cook" mode, adjusting the time to 2 minutes. Once done, quick release the pressure. Stir in lime juice, lime zest, and chopped cilantro. Adjust seasoning if necessary and serve.

## NUTRITIONAL INFORMATION

Per serving: 80 calories, 3g protein, 12g carbohydrates, 3.5g fat, 4g fiber, 0mg cholesterol, 60mg sodium, 500mg potassium.

# Spiced Brussel Sprouts

## INGREDIENTS

- 1 pound Brussel sprouts, trimmed and halved
- 1 tablespoon olive oil
- 1/2 teaspoon ground cumin
- 1/2 teaspoon ground paprika
- 1/4 teaspoon ground turmeric
- 1/4 teaspoon chili powder (adjust to taste)
- Salt and pepper, to taste
- 1/4 cup water
- 1 tablespoon lemon juice (optional for added tang)

 Prep Time: 10 min

 Cook Time: 5 minutes

 Serves: 4

## DIRECTIONS

In a mixing bowl, toss the Brussel sprouts with olive oil, cumin, paprika, turmeric, chili powder, salt, and pepper until evenly coated. Pour the water into the Instant Pot, then add the seasoned Brussel sprouts. Secure the lid and set the Instant Pot to "Manual" or "Pressure Cook" mode, adjusting the time to 2 minutes. Once done, use the quick release method to release the pressure. Drizzle with lemon juice for added tang, stir to combine, and serve hot.

## NUTRITIONAL INFORMATION

Per serving: 90 calories, 4g protein, 16g carbohydrates, 3g fat, 6g fiber, 0mg cholesterol, 30mg sodium, 450mg potassium.

# Creamed Spinach and Artichokes

## INGREDIENTS

- 1 pound fresh spinach, washed and roughly chopped
- 1 can (14 ounces) artichoke hearts, drained and chopped
- 1 cup unsweetened almond milk (or any plant-based milk)
- 1/4 cup nutritional yeast
- 3 cloves garlic, minced
- 1 tablespoon olive oil
- Salt and pepper, to taste
- 1/2 teaspoon nutmeg
- 1/2 cup raw cashews, soaked for 2 hours or boiled for 10 minutes (for creaminess)
- 1/2 cup water

 Prep Time: 15 min

 Cook Time: 10 minutes

 Serves: 4

## DIRECTIONS

Set Instant Pot to "Sauté" mode. Add olive oil and minced garlic. Sauté for 1-2 minutes until aromatic. Add chopped spinach and artichokes, and stir. Sauté for another 2 minutes. In a blender, blend the soaked cashews with water until smooth to create a cashew cream. Add this cream, almond milk, nutritional yeast, nutmeg, salt, and pepper to the Instant Pot. Stir to combine. Close the Instant Pot lid, set to "Manual" or "Pressure Cook" mode, and adjust the time to 5 minutes. After cooking, use the quick release method to release the pressure. Stir well, adjust seasoning if necessary, and serve warm.

## NUTRITIONAL INFORMATION

Per serving: 220 calories, 8g protein, 25g carbohydrates, 12g fat, 7g fiber, 0mg cholesterol, 380mg sodium, 650mg potassium.

# Sweet and Tangy Glazed Carrots

## INGREDIENTS

- 1 pound carrots, peeled and sliced into 1/2-inch pieces
- 1/3 cup pure maple syrup
- 2 tablespoons apple cider vinegar
- 2 tablespoons olive oil
- 1/4 teaspoon ground cinnamon
- Salt and pepper, to taste
- 1 cup water
- 2 tablespoons fresh parsley, finely chopped (optional for garnish)

Prep Time: 10 min

Cook Time: 5 minutes

Serves: 4

## DIRECTIONS

In a mixing bowl, whisk together the maple syrup, apple cider vinegar, olive oil, ground cinnamon, salt, and pepper. Set aside. Add water to the Instant Pot, then place the steaming rack or basket inside. Arrange the sliced carrots on the rack or basket. Secure the Instant Pot lid, set to "Pressure Cook" or "Manual" mode, and adjust the time to 3 minutes. Once done, quickly release the pressure. Remove the carrots and drain the water. Set the Instant Pot to "Sauté" mode and add the previously prepared glaze. Stir until it bubbles and thickens slightly. Add the carrots back into the pot and toss until well-coated with the glaze. Serve warm, garnished with optional chopped parsley.

## NUTRITIONAL INFORMATION

Per serving: 180 calories, 2g protein, 31g carbohydrates, 6g fat, 4g fiber, 0mg cholesterol, 100mg sodium, 400mg potassium.

# Lemon Pepper Asparagus

## INGREDIENTS

- 1 pound fresh asparagus, tough ends trimmed
- 1 cup water
- 2 tablespoons olive oil
- Zest and juice of 1 lemon
- 1 teaspoon freshly ground black pepper
- Salt, to taste

Prep Time: 5 min

Cook Time: 2 minutes

Serves: 4

## DIRECTIONS

Pour the water into the Instant Pot and insert the steamer basket or trivet. Lay the asparagus on the steamer basket or trivet, trying to keep them in a single layer. Close the lid of the Instant Pot and set to "Pressure Cook" or "Manual" for 1 minute. Once cooking is complete, quickly release the pressure. Remove asparagus and toss them in a bowl with olive oil, lemon zest, lemon juice, black pepper, and salt until well coated.

## NUTRITIONAL INFORMATION

Per serving: 70 calories, 2.5g protein, 6g carbohydrates, 5g fat, 2g fiber, 0mg cholesterol, 150mg sodium, 230mg potassium.

# Toasted Sesame Green Beans

## INGREDIENTS

- 1 pound fresh green beans, ends trimmed
- 1 cup water
- 2 tablespoons sesame oil
- 2 tablespoons sesame seeds, toasted
- 1 garlic clove, minced
- Salt, to taste
- 1 tablespoon soy sauce or tamari for a gluten-free option

 Prep Time: 5 min

 Cook Time: 4 minutes

 Serves: 4

## DIRECTIONS

In the Instant Pot, add the water and insert the steamer basket. Place the green beans on the steamer basket. Close the lid of the Instant Pot and set it to "Pressure Cook" or "Manual" for 2 minutes. Once the cooking is complete, quickly release the pressure. In a skillet, heat the sesame oil over medium heat. Add the minced garlic and sauté for a minute until fragrant. Add the steamed green beans, soy sauce, and toss well. Cook for 1-2 minutes. Remove from heat, sprinkle with toasted sesame seeds, and serve immediately.

## NUTRITIONAL INFORMATION

Per serving: 100 calories, 3g protein, 10g carbohydrates, 7g fat, 4g fiber, 0mg cholesterol, 230mg sodium, 240mg potassium.

# Smoky Eggplant Mash

## INGREDIENTS

- 2 medium eggplants, peeled and cubed
- 1 cup water
- 2 garlic cloves, minced
- 2 tablespoons olive oil
- 1 teaspoon smoked paprika
- Salt, to taste
- 1 tablespoon tahini (sesame seed paste)
- 1 tablespoon lemon juice
- Freshly chopped parsley for garnish

 Prep Time: 10 min

 Cook Time: 12 minutes

 Serves: 4

## DIRECTIONS

In the Instant Pot, add water followed by the cubed eggplants. Close the lid, set the vent to "Sealing", and pressure cook on high for 10 minutes. Once done, quickly release the pressure. Drain the cooked eggplant and return it to the Instant Pot. Add garlic, olive oil, smoked paprika, tahini, and lemon juice. Mash the mixture using a potato masher or fork until smooth. Adjust seasoning as per taste and transfer the mash to a serving bowl. Garnish with freshly chopped parsley before serving.

## NUTRITIONAL INFORMATION

Per serving: 130 calories, 3g protein, 15g carbohydrates, 7g fat, 7g fiber, 0mg cholesterol, 80mg sodium, 390mg potassium.

# Turmeric Infused Quinoa

## INGREDIENTS

- 1 cup quinoa, rinsed and drained
- 1 ¾ cups water or vegetable broth
- 1 tablespoon olive oil
- 2 garlic cloves, minced
- 1 teaspoon ground turmeric
- 1/2 teaspoon black pepper
- Salt, to taste
- Freshly chopped cilantro or parsley for garnish (optional)

 Prep Time: 5 min

 Cook Time: 12 minutes

 Serves: 4

## DIRECTIONS

Turn on the Instant Pot to the sauté mode and heat the olive oil. Add the minced garlic and sauté for about 1 minute until fragrant. Stir in the quinoa, turmeric, black pepper, and salt, ensuring the quinoa grains are well coated with the spices. Add water or vegetable broth and give everything a quick stir. Close the lid, set the vent to "Sealing", and pressure cook on high for 1 minute. Once done, let the pressure release naturally for 10 minutes, then quickly release any remaining pressure. Fluff the cooked quinoa with a fork, garnish with chopped cilantro or parsley, and serve.

## NUTRITIONAL INFORMATION

Per serving: 210 calories, 8g protein, 37g carbohydrates, 3.5g fat, 3g fiber, 0mg cholesterol, 10mg sodium, 320mg potassium.

# Buttery Garlic Broccoli

## INGREDIENTS

- 4 cups broccoli florets (about 2 medium heads)
- 3 tablespoons plant-based butter (e.g., almond or cashew-based)
- 4 garlic cloves, minced
- 1/4 cup water or vegetable broth
- Salt and pepper to taste
- A squeeze of fresh lemon juice (optional)
- Red chili flakes (optional, for a hint of spice)

 Prep Time: 10 min

 Cook Time: 3 minutes

 Serves: 4

## DIRECTIONS

Add the water or vegetable broth to the Instant Pot. Place the broccoli florets in a steam basket inside the pot. Close the Instant Pot lid, set the vent to "Sealing", and steam the broccoli on high pressure for 0 minutes. Once done, quickly release the pressure. In a separate pan or on sauté mode in the Instant Pot, melt the plant-based butter. Add the minced garlic and sauté until golden and fragrant. Mix the buttery garlic mixture with the steamed broccoli, tossing well to ensure the florets are well-coated. Season with salt, pepper, and optionally with lemon juice and chili flakes.

## NUTRITIONAL INFORMATION

Per serving: 95 calories, 3g protein, 10g carbohydrates, 6g fat, 3g fiber, 0mg cholesterol, 90mg sodium, 350mg potassium.

# Moroccan Spiced Couscous

## INGREDIENTS

- 1 1/2 cups couscous
- 1 3/4 cups vegetable broth or water
- 2 tablespoons olive oil or plant-based butter
- 1 onion, finely chopped
- 2 garlic cloves, minced
- 1/4 cup raisins or dried currants
- 1/4 cup chopped dried apricots
- 1 teaspoon ground cumin
- 1/2 teaspoon ground turmeric
- 1/2 teaspoon ground cinnamon

Prep Time: 10 min

Cook Time: 5 minutes

Serves: 4

## DIRECTIONS

Turn the Instant Pot to sauté mode and heat the olive oil or plant-based butter. Add the onions and garlic, sautéing until translucent. Stir in the ground cumin, ground turmeric, ground cinnamon, raisins, and dried apricots. Continue to sauté for another 1-2 minutes until fragrant. Pour in the vegetable broth or water and bring to a simmer. Stir in the couscous, ensuring it's fully submerged in the liquid. Seal the Instant Pot lid and set to manual high pressure for 2 minutes. Once done, let it release naturally for 2 minutes, then perform a quick release. Fluff the couscous with a fork and stir in the fresh parsley and mint. Season with salt and pepper to taste.

## NUTRITIONAL INFORMATION

Per serving: 320 calories, 8g protein, 62g carbohydrates, 5g fat, 4g fiber, 0mg cholesterol, 180mg sodium, 230mg potassium.

# Ginger Glazed Snap Peas

## INGREDIENTS

- 1 lb fresh snap peas, trimmed
- 1 tablespoon olive oil
- 3 tablespoons fresh ginger, grated
- 2 tablespoons maple syrup or agave nectar
- 2 tablespoons soy sauce or tamari (for gluten-free option)
- 1 teaspoon toasted sesame oil
- 1 tablespoon toasted sesame seeds (optional)
- Salt to taste

Prep Time: 10 min

Cook Time: 3 minutes

Serves: 4

## DIRECTIONS

Turn the Instant Pot to sauté mode and heat the olive oil. Add the grated ginger and sauté for about 1 minute until aromatic. Stir in the maple syrup and soy sauce, simmering for 1-2 minutes to meld the flavors. Add the snap peas to the pot, stirring well to coat them with the ginger glaze. Seal the Instant Pot lid, and set to steam mode for 1 minute. Once done, perform a quick release. Drizzle with toasted sesame oil, garnish with sesame seeds if desired, and season with salt to taste.

## NUTRITIONAL INFORMATION

Per serving: 110 calories, 3g protein, 18g carbohydrates, 3g fat, 3g fiber, 0mg cholesterol, 520mg sodium, 250mg potassium.

# Herbed Potato Salad

## INGREDIENTS

- 1.5 lbs baby potatoes, halved
- 1 cup vegetable broth or water
- 1/3 cup vegan mayonnaise
- 1 tablespoon Dijon mustard
- 2 tablespoons fresh parsley, finely chopped
- 1 tablespoon fresh dill, finely chopped
- 1 tablespoon fresh chives, finely chopped
- 2 green onions, thinly sliced
- 1 celery stalk, finely diced
- Salt and pepper to taste
- Juice of half a lemon

Prep Time: 15 min

Cook Time: 7 minutes

Serves: 4

## DIRECTIONS

Add baby potatoes and vegetable broth or water to the Instant Pot. Secure the lid and set to high pressure for 7 minutes. Once done, perform a quick release and drain the potatoes. In a large mixing bowl, combine vegan mayonnaise, Dijon mustard, parsley, dill, chives, green onions, celery, salt, pepper, and lemon juice. Mix until well combined. Gently fold in the cooked potatoes until they are well-coated with the herbed dressing. Chill the potato salad for at least an hour before serving for the best flavor.

## NUTRITIONAL INFORMATION

Per serving: 240 calories, 3g protein, 40g carbohydrates, 8g fat, 4g fiber, 0mg cholesterol, 400mg sodium, 900mg potassium.

Main Dish Marvels

# Chickpea Coconut Curry

## INGREDIENTS

- 2 cans (15 oz each) chickpeas, drained and rinsed
- 1 can (13.5 oz) full-fat coconut milk
- 1 large onion, diced
- 3 cloves garlic, minced
- 1-inch fresh ginger, grated
- 2 tablespoons tomato paste
- 2 tablespoons curry powder
- 1 teaspoon turmeric
- 1 teaspoon cumin
- 1/2 teaspoon red chili flakes (adjust to taste)
- 1 cup vegetable broth or water

 Prep Time: 15 min

 Cook Time: 20 minutes

 Serves: 4

## DIRECTIONS

Set the Instant Pot to "Sauté" mode and add coconut or olive oil. Once hot, sauté onions, garlic, and ginger until translucent. Add tomato paste, curry powder, turmeric, cumin, and red chili flakes. Stir until the spices are fragrant. Add chickpeas, coconut milk, and vegetable broth or water. Stir to combine. Secure the lid and set the Instant Pot to "Manual" or "Pressure Cook" on high pressure for 15 minutes. Once done, allow the pressure to release naturally for 5 minutes, then perform a quick release. Garnish with fresh cilantro before serving. It pairs wonderfully with rice or naan.

## NUTRITIONAL INFORMATION

Per serving: 460 calories, 15g protein, 58g carbohydrates, 20g fat, 12g fiber, 0mg cholesterol, 800mg sodium, 800mg potassium.

# Stuffed Acorn Squash

## INGREDIENTS

- 2 medium acorn squashes, halved and seeds removed
- 1 cup quinoa, rinsed and drained
- 2 cups vegetable broth
- 1 medium onion, diced
- 2 cloves garlic, minced
- 1 cup kale, chopped
- 1/2 cup dried cranberries or raisins
- 1/2 cup chopped walnuts or pecans
- 2 tablespoons olive oil or coconut oil
- 1 teaspoon ground sage
- 1 teaspoon thyme
- Salt and pepper to taste

 Prep Time: 20 min

 Cook Time: 25 minutes

Serves: 4

## DIRECTIONS

In the Instant Pot, cook quinoa with vegetable broth for 5 mins on high pressure. After quick release, transfer quinoa to a bowl. In "Sauté" mode, heat oil, sauté onions and garlic until translucent. Add kale, cranberries/raisins, nuts, sage, thyme, salt, and pepper; stir for a few minutes. Combine with cooked quinoa. Stuff each acorn squash half with the quinoa mixture. In the Instant Pot, pour 1 cup of water, place the trivet inside, and arrange stuffed squash. Secure the lid, set to "Manual" or "Pressure Cook" for 20 mins on high pressure. Afterward, allow natural pressure release.

## NUTRITIONAL INFORMATION

Per serving: 380 calories, 9g protein, 60g carbohydrates, 14g fat, 8g fiber, 0mg cholesterol, 320mg sodium, 900mg potassium.

# BBQ Jackfruit Tacos

## INGREDIENTS

- 2 cans (20 oz each) young green jackfruit in water, drained and rinsed
- 1 medium onion, finely chopped
- 3 cloves garlic, minced
- 1 1/2 cups BBQ sauce (plant-based and without added sugars)
- 1 cup vegetable broth
- 1 tablespoon olive oil
- 2 teaspoons smoked paprika
- 1 teaspoon ground cumin
- 1/2 teaspoon chili powder
- 8 taco-sized tortillas

 Prep Time: 15 min

 Cook Time: 25 minutes

 Serves: 4

## DIRECTIONS

Set the Instant Pot to "Sauté" mode. Add olive oil, onions, and garlic. Sauté until the onions become translucent. Add the drained jackfruit to the pot and sauté for another 3-4 minutes, using a fork or spatula to break apart the jackfruit to mimic shredded meat. Stir in the smoked paprika, ground cumin, chili powder, BBQ sauce, and vegetable broth. Secure the lid and set the Instant Pot to "Manual" or "Pressure Cook" for 20 minutes on high pressure. After cooking, perform a quick release. Assemble your tacos by placing the BBQ jackfruit mixture onto each tortilla, and top with your desired toppings.

## NUTRITIONAL INFORMATION

Per serving: 410 calories, 5g protein, 85g carbohydrates, 5g fat, 6g fiber, 0mg cholesterol, 750mg sodium, 500mg potassium.

# Lentil and Vegetable Paella

## INGREDIENTS

- 1 cup green lentils, rinsed and drained
- 1 cup paella rice or short-grain rice
- 2 1/2 cups vegetable broth
- 1 medium onion, chopped
- 1 bell pepper, sliced
- 1 zucchini, diced
- 3 cloves garlic, minced
- 1/2 cup frozen green peas, thawed
- 1/4 cup fresh parsley, chopped
- 1/4 cup fresh lemon juice
- 1 teaspoon smoked paprika, turmeric
- 1/2 teaspoon saffron threads (optional)

 Prep Time: 20 min

 Cook Time: 25 minutes

 Serves: 4

## DIRECTIONS

Set the Instant Pot to "Sauté" mode and add the olive oil. Once heated, add the onion and garlic, and sauté until translucent. Stir in the bell pepper, zucchini, smoked paprika, turmeric, and saffron threads, and cook for another 3 minutes. Add the lentils, rice, and vegetable broth, stirring well to combine. Secure the lid. Set the Instant Pot to "Manual" or "Pressure Cook" mode and cook on high pressure for 20 minutes. Once done, allow a natural release for 10 minutes, then perform a quick release. Stir in the green peas, fresh parsley, and lemon juice. Season with salt and pepper to taste before serving.

## NUTRITIONAL INFORMATION

Per serving: 380 calories, 15g protein, 70g carbohydrates, 7g fat, 16g fiber, 0mg cholesterol, 450mg sodium, 700mg potassium.

# Sweet and Sour Tempeh

## INGREDIENTS

- 8 oz tempeh, cubed
- 1 red bell pepper, sliced
- 1 green bell pepper, sliced
- 1 medium onion, chopped
- 3 cloves garlic, minced
- 1/2 cup pineapple chunks (fresh or canned)
- 1/4 cup apple cider vinegar
- 3 tablespoons soy sauce or tamari, maple syrup
- 1 tablespoon cornstarch mixed with 1 tablespoon water
- 2 tablespoons tomato paste
- 1/2 cup water or vegetable broth

 Prep Time: 15 min

 Cook Time: 20 minutes

 Serves: 4

## DIRECTIONS

In Instant Pot's "Sauté" mode, heat olive oil and brown tempeh cubes for 3-4 mins. Add onion, garlic, bell peppers, and pineapple; sauté for another 2 mins. In a bowl, whisk together apple cider vinegar, soy sauce, maple syrup, cornstarch mixture, tomato paste, and water. Pour over tempeh and veggies. Secure the lid, set to "Manual" or "Pressure Cook" for 10 mins on high pressure. After cooking, natural release for 5 mins, then quick release. Stir well, garnish with green onions, and serve with rice or noodles.

## NUTRITIONAL INFORMATION

Per serving: 210 calories, 13g protein, 30g carbohydrates, 6g fat, 2g fiber, 0mg cholesterol, 570mg sodium, 460mg potassium.

# Instant Pot Vegetable Korma

## INGREDIENTS

- 1 medium onion, finely chopped
- 3 garlic cloves, minced
- 1-inch ginger, grated
- 2 medium carrots, chopped
- 1 cup cauliflower florets, green beans, cut into 1-inch pieces
- 1 bell pepper, chopped
- 2 medium potatoes, diced
- 1/2 cup green peas
- 1 can (14 oz) coconut milk
- 1/4 cup cashews, soaked and blended to a paste
- 2 tablespoons tomato paste
- 1 teaspoon garam masala, turmeric powder, cumin powder

  Prep Time: 20 min

 Cook Time: 15 minutes

 Serves: 4

## DIRECTIONS

Set the Instant Pot to "Sauté" mode. Melt the coconut oil, then add onions, garlic, and ginger. Sauté until onions are translucent. Add in the spices (garam masala, turmeric, cumin, and red chili powder), followed by the tomato paste. Mix well. Stir in the vegetables (carrots, cauliflower, green beans, bell pepper, potatoes, and peas). Pour in the coconut milk and stir. Secure the lid, set the Instant Pot to "Pressure Cook" or "Manual" mode, and cook on high for 10 minutes. Allow a natural release for 5 minutes, then perform a quick release. Stir in the cashew paste, adjust seasoning if needed, then garnish with cilantro and almond slices. Serve with rice or flatbread.

## NUTRITIONAL INFORMATION

Per serving: 410 calories, 9g protein, 45g carbohydrates, 24g fat, 8g fiber, 0mg cholesterol, 180mg sodium, 750mg potassium.

# Teriyaki Tofu Stir-Fry

## INGREDIENTS

- 1 block (14 oz) firm tofu, drained, pressed, and cubed
- 3 tablespoons soy sauce or tamari
- 3 tablespoons maple syrup or agave nectar
- 1 tablespoon rice vinegar, minced ginger
- 2 garlic cloves, minced
- 1 tablespoon cornstarch mixed with 2 tablespoons water
- 2 tablespoons sesame oil or neutral oil
- 1 cup broccoli florets
- 1 bell pepper, sliced
- 1 medium carrot, julienned
- 1/2 cup snap peas

 Prep Time: 20 min

 Cook Time: 10 minutes

Serves: 4

## DIRECTIONS

In a bowl, whisk together soy sauce, maple syrup, rice vinegar, ginger, garlic, and cornstarch slurry. Set aside. Set the Instant Pot to "Sauté" mode. Add the oil. Once heated, add the tofu cubes and sauté until they're lightly browned on all sides. Pour the teriyaki sauce mixture over the tofu, ensuring that all tofu pieces are coated. Add broccoli, bell pepper, carrot, and snap peas. Stir gently.
Close the Instant Pot lid, set it to "Manual" or "Pressure Cook" mode, and cook on high pressure for 2 minutes. Once done, quick release the pressure. Stir the mixture, adjust seasoning if necessary. Serve hot, garnished with green onions and sesame seeds.

## NUTRITIONAL INFORMATION

Per serving: 250 calories, 12g protein, 29g carbohydrates, 10g fat, 4g fiber, 0mg cholesterol, 750mg sodium, 400mg potassium.

# Mushroom and Spinach Stroganoff

## INGREDIENTS

- 1 tablespoon olive oil
- 1 large onion, finely chopped
- 3 garlic cloves, minced
- 1 pound cremini or button mushrooms, sliced
- 3 cups fresh spinach, roughly chopped
- 1 cup vegetable broth
- 1 tablespoon soy sauce or tamari
- 1 tablespoon Dijon mustard
- 1/4 cup cashew cream or vegan sour cream
- 1 teaspoon smoked paprika
- 2 tablespoons fresh parsley, chopped for garnish

 Prep Time: 15 min

 Cook Time: 10 minutes

Serves: 4

## DIRECTIONS

Set the Instant Pot to "Sauté" mode and add olive oil. Once heated, add onions and garlic. Sauté until the onions are translucent. Add sliced mushrooms and cook until they release their juices and start to brown. Stir in spinach, vegetable broth, soy sauce, Dijon mustard, and smoked paprika. Adjust seasoning with salt and pepper. Close the Instant Pot lid, set it to "Manual" or "Pressure Cook" mode, and cook on high pressure for 5 minutes. Once done, quick release the pressure. Open the lid, stir in the cashew cream, and adjust seasoning if necessary. Serve over pasta or rice, garnished with fresh parsley.

## NUTRITIONAL INFORMATION

Per serving: 210 calories, 7g protein, 25g carbohydrates, 10g fat, 4g fiber, 0mg cholesterol, 450mg sodium, 600mg potassium.

# Hearty Vegetable Tagine

## INGREDIENTS

- 1 large onion, chopped
- 3 garlic cloves, minced
- 1 large carrot, diced
- 1 bell pepper, diced
- 2 medium zucchinis, diced
- 1 can (14 oz) chickpeas, drained and rinsed, diced tomatoes
- 1/4 cup dried apricots, chopped
- 2 teaspoons ground cumin, ground coriander
- 1 teaspoon ground cinnamon
- 1/2 teaspoon turmeric, cayenne pepper
- 1 cup vegetable broth

 Prep Time: 20 min

 Cook Time: 25 minutes

 Serves: 4

## DIRECTIONS

Set the Instant Pot to "Sauté" mode. Add olive oil, onion, and garlic. Sauté until the onion is translucent. Add carrots, bell pepper, and zucchinis. Continue sautéing for another 3 minutes. Stir in chickpeas, diced tomatoes, dried apricots, spices, and vegetable broth. Season with salt and pepper. Lock the Instant Pot lid in place. Set the pot to "Manual" or "Pressure Cook" mode and cook on high pressure for 20 minutes. Once done, allow a natural pressure release for 5 minutes, followed by a quick release. Serve the tagine garnished with fresh cilantro or parsley and toasted slivered almonds.

## NUTRITIONAL INFORMATION

Per serving: 310 calories, 11g protein, 45g carbohydrates, 12g fat, 10g fiber, 0mg cholesterol, 530mg sodium, 800mg potassium.

# Zesty Lemon Seitan Platter

## INGREDIENTS

- 1 pound seitan, sliced into bite-sized pieces
- 1 tablespoon olive oil
- 3 garlic cloves, minced
- Zest and juice of 2 lemons
- 1 tablespoon soy sauce or tamari (low sodium)
- 1 teaspoon dried oregano
- 1/4 teaspoon black pepper
- 1 cup vegetable broth
- 1 bell pepper, sliced (any color)
- 1 large onion, thinly sliced
- 1 cup cherry tomatoes, halved
- Fresh parsley, for garnish

 Prep Time: 15 min

 Cook Time: 25 minutes

 Serves: 4

## DIRECTIONS

In a bowl, combine lemon zest, lemon juice, soy sauce, oregano, and black pepper. Mix well and add the seitan pieces, ensuring they're well coated. Marinate for 10 minutes. Set the Instant Pot to "Sauté" mode. Add olive oil, garlic, bell pepper, and onion. Sauté until the onion is translucent. Add the marinated seitan along with the marinade and vegetable broth to the pot. Give it a gentle stir. Lock the Instant Pot lid in place. Set the pot to "Manual" or "Pressure Cook" mode and cook on high pressure for 20 minutes. Allow a natural pressure release for 5 minutes, followed by a quick release. Stir in cherry tomatoes, serve on a platter, and garnish with fresh parsley.

## NUTRITIONAL INFORMATION

Per serving: 250 calories, 25g protein, 15g carbohydrates, 9g fat, 3g fiber, 0mg cholesterol, 420mg sodium, 500mg potassium.

# Moroccan Vegetable Stew

## INGREDIENTS

- 2 tablespoons olive oil
- 1 large onion, chopped
- 3 garlic cloves, minced
- 2 carrots, chopped
- 1 bell pepper, chopped
- 1 zucchini, chopped
- 1 cup chickpeas
- 2 cups diced tomatoes
- 4 cups vegetable broth
- 1 teaspoon ground cumin, coriander
- 1/2 teaspoon ground turmeric, paprika
- 1/4 teaspoon ground cinnamon
- 1 bay leaf

 Prep Time: 20 min

 Cook Time: 25 minutes

Serves: 4 servings

## DIRECTIONS

Set the Instant Pot to the "Sauté" mode. Add olive oil, followed by onions and garlic. Sauté until the onions are translucent. Add the carrots, bell pepper, zucchini, and spices (cumin, coriander, turmeric, cinnamon, and paprika). Stir well to combine. Add chickpeas, diced tomatoes, vegetable broth, bay leaf, salt, and pepper. Mix well. Close the Instant Pot lid and set it to "Manual" or "Pressure Cook" mode. Cook on high pressure for 20 minutes. Allow a natural release for 10 minutes, then do a quick release. Serve hot, garnished with fresh cilantro or parsley.

## NUTRITIONAL INFORMATION

Per serving: 220 calories, 8g protein, 35g carbohydrates, 7g fat, 9g fiber, 0mg cholesterol, 500mg sodium, 750mg potassium.

# BBQ Lentil Meatballs

## INGREDIENTS

- 1 cup dried green lentils, rinsed and drained
- 2.5 cups vegetable broth
- 1 small onion, finely chopped
- 3 garlic cloves, minced
- 1 cup breadcrumbs (ensure plant-based if store-bought)
- 2 tablespoons flaxseed meal mixed with 5 tablespoons water (flax egg)
- 1 teaspoon smoked paprika
- 1/4 cup chopped fresh parsley
- 1 cup BBQ sauce

 Prep Time: 15 min

 Cook Time: 30 minutes

 Serves: 4

## DIRECTIONS

In the Instant Pot, combine lentils and vegetable broth. Pressure cook on high for 15 mins with natural release. Transfer cooked lentils to a bowl, let cool. Add onion, garlic, breadcrumbs, flax egg, smoked paprika, pepper, salt, and parsley to the lentils. Mix well and shape into balls. Place back in the Instant Pot, pour BBQ sauce over them. In "Sauté" mode, cook for 10 mins, stirring occasionally. Serve hot with extra BBQ sauce if desired.

## NUTRITIONAL INFORMATION

Per serving: 320 calories, 15g protein, 58g carbohydrates, 4g fat, 17g fiber, 0mg cholesterol, 820mg sodium, 600mg potassium.

# Creamy Cauliflower Curry

## INGREDIENTS

- 1 large cauliflower, cut into florets
- 1 can (14 oz.) full-fat coconut milk
- 1 large onion, finely chopped
- 3 cloves garlic, minced
- 2 tablespoons coconut oil or olive oil
- 2 tablespoons curry powder
- 1 teaspoon ground turmeric
- 1 teaspoon ground cumin
- 1/2 teaspoon chili powder (adjust to taste)
- 1/2 cup vegetable broth or water

Prep Time: 15 min

Cook Time: 20 minutes

Serves: 4

## DIRECTIONS

Set the Instant Pot to "Sauté" mode and heat the oil. Add the chopped onions and garlic, sautéing until translucent. Stir in the curry powder, turmeric, cumin, and chili powder, ensuring the onion and garlic are coated and fragrant. Add the cauliflower florets to the pot and stir to coat them with the spice mixture.

Pour in the vegetable broth or water, followed by the coconut milk. Mix well, then close the Instant Pot lid, set the valve to "sealing", and cook on high pressure for 5 minutes. Once done, release the pressure naturally. Adjust seasoning if necessary and serve hot, garnished with fresh cilantro.

## NUTRITIONAL INFORMATION

Per serving: 310 calories, 7g protein, 20g carbohydrates, 25g fat, 5g fiber, 0mg cholesterol, 220mg sodium, 750mg potassium.

# Seitan Pepper Steak

## INGREDIENTS

- 1 lb seitan, sliced
- 3 bell peppers
- 1 large onion, sliced
- 3 cloves garlic, minced
- 2 tablespoons soy sauce or tamari
- 1 tablespoon vegan Worcestershire sauce
- 1/2 cup vegetable broth
- 2 tablespoons cornstarch mixed with 2 tablespoons water (cornstarch slurry)

Prep Time: 20 min

Cook Time: 15 minutes

Serves: 4 servings

## DIRECTIONS

In the Instant Pot's "Sauté" mode, heat oil and sauté sliced seitan strips until slightly browned. Add garlic, onions, and bell peppers; sauté for 2-3 mins. In a small bowl, mix soy sauce, Worcestershire sauce, and vegetable broth. Pour over seitan and veggies in the Instant Pot. Secure the lid, set to "Manual" on high for 10 mins. After cooking, quick release pressure. In "Sauté" mode, stir in cornstarch slurry. Cook for 2-3 mins until the sauce thickens. Adjust seasoning. Serve hot, garnished with sesame seeds and sliced green onions if desired.

## NUTRITIONAL INFORMATION

Per serving: 250 calories, 25g protein, 20g carbohydrates, 8g fat, 4g fiber, 0mg cholesterol, 600mg sodium, 500mg potassium.

# Thai Basil Vegetable Medley

## INGREDIENTS

- 1 cup broccoli florets
- 1 red bell pepper, sliced
- 1 yellow bell pepper, sliced
- 1 zucchini, sliced into half-moons
- 1 carrot, thinly sliced
- 2 cups snap peas
- 1 cup mushrooms, sliced
- 3 cloves garlic, minced
- 1 small red chili, sliced (optional for heat)
- 2 tablespoons soy sauce or tamari
- 1 tablespoon coconut sugar or brown sugar
- 1/2 cup vegetable broth
- 1 tablespoon coconut oil
- 1 cup fresh Thai basil leaves
- 1 tablespoon lime juice
- Salt to taste

Prep Time: 20 min

Cook Time: 8 minutes

Serves: 4 servings

## DIRECTIONS

Turn on the Instant Pot's "Sauté" mode and melt the coconut oil. Add garlic, and red chili (if using), sautéing for about 1 minute until fragrant. Add all the vegetables to the pot and stir for another 1-2 minutes. In a separate bowl, combine the soy sauce, coconut sugar, and vegetable broth. Pour this mixture over the vegetables in the Instant Pot. Secure the Instant Pot lid, set the valve to "sealing", and cook on manual/high pressure for 5 minutes. After cooking, perform a quick release. Once pressure is fully released, open the lid, stir in Thai basil leaves and lime juice. Adjust seasoning if necessary before serving.

## NUTRITIONAL INFORMATION

Per serving: 140 calories, 5g protein, 23g carbohydrates, 3g fat, 5g fiber, 0mg cholesterol, 500mg sodium, 600mg potassium.

Sauces,
Salsas, &
Spreads

# Creamy Avocado Lime Sauce

## INGREDIENTS

- 2 ripe avocados, peeled and pitted
- Juice and zest of 2 limes
- 2 cloves garlic
- 1/2 cup unsweetened almond milk (or other plant-based milk)
- 1/4 cup fresh cilantro, chopped
- 1/2 teaspoon sea salt
- 1/4 teaspoon black pepper
- 1/4 teaspoon cumin
- 1/2 cup vegetable broth

Prep Time: 10 min

Cook Time: 5 minutes

Serves: 4

## DIRECTIONS

Combine avocados, lime juice, lime zest, garlic, almond milk, cilantro, salt, pepper, and cumin in a blender or food processor. Blend until smooth. Pour the mixture into the Instant Pot and add the vegetable broth. Set the Instant Pot to "Sauté" mode and cook the mixture, stirring frequently until heated through, about 4-5 minutes. Turn off the Instant Pot, taste, and adjust seasoning if necessary. Use immediately or store in an airtight container in the refrigerator for up to 2 days.

## NUTRITIONAL INFORMATION

Per serving: 170 calories, 2g protein, 12g carbohydrates, 14g fat, 7g fiber, 0mg cholesterol, 320mg sodium, 500mg potassium.

# Zesty Tomato Salsa

## INGREDIENTS

- 5 ripe tomatoes, diced
- 1 white onion, diced
- 3 cloves garlic, minced
- 1 jalapeño, seeds removed and finely diced
- Juice of 1 lime
- 1/2 cup fresh cilantro, chopped
- 1 teaspoon sea salt
- 1/2 teaspoon ground black pepper
- 1/2 cup vegetable broth

Prep Time: 10 min

Cook Time: 5 minutes

Serves: 4 servings

## DIRECTIONS

Add the tomatoes, onion, garlic, jalapeño, lime juice, cilantro, salt, and pepper to the Instant Pot. Pour in the vegetable broth and gently mix all the ingredients. Set the Instant Pot to "Sauté" mode and cook for about 5 minutes, stirring occasionally. After cooking, turn off the Instant Pot and let the salsa cool for a bit before transferring to a container. Adjust seasoning if necessary.

## NUTRITIONAL INFORMATION

Per serving: 40 calories, 1g protein, 9g carbohydrates, 0.2g fat, 2g fiber, 0mg cholesterol, 600mg sodium, 300mg potassium.

# Roasted Red Pepper Spread

## INGREDIENTS

- 4 large red bell peppers, seeded and quartered
- 2 cloves garlic, minced
- 1 tablespoon olive oil
- 1/4 cup toasted walnuts
- 2 tablespoons nutritional yeast
- Juice of 1 lemon
- 1/4 teaspoon smoked paprika
- Salt and pepper to taste

Prep Time: 15 min

Cook Time: 12 minutes

Serves: 4

## DIRECTIONS

Place the red bell peppers and garlic in the Instant Pot. Drizzle with olive oil and toss to coat. Set the Instant Pot to "Sauté" mode and roast the peppers for about 10 minutes, or until they're slightly charred, stirring occasionally. Once roasted, turn off the Instant Pot. Add toasted walnuts, nutritional yeast, lemon juice, smoked paprika, salt, and pepper to the pot. Blend the mixture using an immersion blender until smooth. If the consistency is too thick, you can add a bit of water or olive oil to achieve your desired texture.

## NUTRITIONAL INFORMATION

Per serving: 120 calories, 4g protein, 10g carbohydrates, 8g fat, 3g fiber, 0mg cholesterol, 50mg sodium, 290mg potassium.

# Instant Pot Marinara

## INGREDIENTS

- 1 tablespoon olive oil
- 1 medium onion, finely chopped
- 3 cloves garlic, minced
- 1 (28-ounce) can of whole tomatoes (preferably San Marzano)
- 1 teaspoon dried basil
- 1 teaspoon dried oregano
- 1/2 teaspoon dried thyme
- 1/4 teaspoon red pepper flakes (optional for a bit of heat)
- 2 bay leaves
- Salt and pepper, to taste
- 1 teaspoon sugar (optional, to taste)

Prep Time: 10 min

Cook Time: 25 minutes

Serves: 4 servings

## DIRECTIONS

Turn the Instant Pot to the "Sauté" function. Add olive oil, onion, and garlic. Sauté until the onion is translucent, about 3-4 minutes. Add the whole tomatoes, crushing them with your hands as you add them to the pot. Stir in basil, oregano, thyme, red pepper flakes (if using), bay leaves, salt, and pepper.

Close the Instant Pot lid and set to "Manual" or "Pressure Cook" on high pressure for 20 minutes. Once the cooking is done, let the pressure naturally release for 10 minutes, then manually release any remaining pressure. Remove the bay leaves. If desired, use an immersion blender for a smoother sauce or leave as is for a chunkier consistency. Adjust seasoning with salt, pepper, and sugar if needed.

## NUTRITIONAL INFORMATION

Per serving: 90 calories, 2g protein, 15g carbohydrates, 3g fat, 3g fiber, 0mg cholesterol, 300mg sodium, 400mg potassium.

# Almond Herb Pesto

## INGREDIENTS

- 1 cup fresh basil leaves, packed
- 1 cup fresh parsley leaves, packed
- 1/2 cup almonds, toasted
- 3 cloves garlic
- 1/4 cup nutritional yeast (as a plant-based alternative to parmesan)
- 1/2 cup extra virgin olive oil
- Juice of 1 lemon
- Salt and pepper, to taste

Prep Time: 10 min

Cook Time: 5 minutes

Serves: 4

## DIRECTIONS

Turn the Instant Pot on to the "Sauté" function. Add almonds and toast for about 3-4 minutes, or until they are lightly golden. Remove and let cool. In a food processor or blender, combine the toasted almonds, basil, parsley, garlic, and nutritional yeast. Pulse until the ingredients are finely chopped. With the machine running, slowly add in the olive oil and lemon juice. Continue blending until the pesto reaches a smooth consistency. Season with salt and pepper to taste. If it's too thick, add a bit more olive oil or a splash of water.

## NUTRITIONAL INFORMATION

Per serving: 310 calories, 5g protein, 7g carbohydrates, 31g fat, 3g fiber, 0mg cholesterol, 50mg sodium, 200mg potassium.

# Mango Pineapple Salsa

## INGREDIENTS

- 1 ripe mango, peeled and diced
- 1 cup fresh pineapple, diced
- 1/4 cup red onion, finely chopped
- 1/4 cup fresh cilantro, chopped
- 1 jalapeño, seeds removed and finely chopped (optional for some heat)
- Juice of 1 lime
- Salt and pepper, to taste

Prep Time: 15 min

Cook Time: 0 minutes

Serves: 4

## DIRECTIONS

In a large mixing bowl, combine diced mango, pineapple, red onion, cilantro, and jalapeño (if using). Squeeze the juice of the lime over the ingredients in the bowl and mix well. Season with salt and pepper to taste. Let the salsa sit for 10 minutes to meld flavors together, then serve.

## NUTRITIONAL INFORMATION

Per serving: 70 calories, 1g protein, 18g carbohydrates, 0.5g fat, 2g fiber, 0mg cholesterol, 150mg sodium, 200mg potassium.

# Spicy Chipotle Dressing

## INGREDIENTS

- 1 cup unsweetened plant-based yogurt (e.g., almond, soy, or coconut yogurt)
- 2 chipotle peppers in adobo sauce
- 2 cloves garlic
- Juice of 1 lime
- 1 tablespoon agave nectar or maple syrup
- 1 tablespoon apple cider vinegar
- 1/2 teaspoon smoked paprika
- Salt and pepper, to taste

Prep Time: 10 min

Cook Time: 0 minutes

Serves: 4

## DIRECTIONS

In a blender or food processor, combine the plant-based yogurt, chipotle peppers, garlic, lime juice, agave nectar, apple cider vinegar, and smoked paprika. Blend until the mixture is smooth and creamy. Season with salt and pepper to taste. Transfer to a container and refrigerate for at least an hour before serving to allow flavors to meld.

## NUTRITIONAL INFORMATION

Per serving: 70 calories, 2g protein, 10g carbohydrates, 2g fat, 1g fiber, 0mg cholesterol, 250mg sodium, 150mg potassium.

# Walnut and Basil Spread

## INGREDIENTS

- 1 cup walnuts
- 2 cups fresh basil leaves
- 3 cloves garlic, minced
- 1/4 cup nutritional yeast
- Juice of 1 lemon
- 1/3 cup extra-virgin olive oil
- Salt and pepper, to taste

Prep Time: 10 min

Cook Time: 0 minutes

Serves: 4 servings

## DIRECTIONS

In a food processor, combine the walnuts, basil, garlic, nutritional yeast, and lemon juice. Pulse until the mixture is coarsely ground. While the processor is running, slowly drizzle in the olive oil until the mixture becomes creamy. Season with salt and pepper to taste. Transfer the spread to a container and refrigerate. Allow flavors to meld for at least an hour before serving.

## NUTRITIONAL INFORMATION

Per serving: 320 calories, 7g protein, 8g carbohydrates, 30g fat, 3g fiber, 0mg cholesterol, 10mg sodium, 300mg potassium.

# Cashew Queso Dip

## INGREDIENTS

- 1 cup raw cashews (soaked for 4 hours or overnight, then drained)
- 1/2 cup water
- 1/4 cup nutritional yeast
- 1 small roasted red pepper (skin removed)
- 2 cloves garlic, minced
- 1 teaspoon onion powder
- 1 teaspoon smoked paprika
- 1/2 teaspoon turmeric powder
- 1/2 teaspoon cayenne pepper (adjust to taste)
- Juice of 1 lime
- Salt, to taste

Prep Time: 15 min

Cook Time: 5 minutes

Serves: 4

## DIRECTIONS

In the Instant Pot, add soaked cashews and water. Set to "Sauté" mode for 3 minutes, stirring occasionally to soften the cashews further. Once softened, turn off the Instant Pot and allow cashews to cool slightly. Transfer the softened cashews and the remaining water to a blender. Add all other ingredients. Blend until smooth and creamy. Taste and adjust seasoning if necessary.

## NUTRITIONAL INFORMATION

Per serving: 210 calories, 8g protein, 12g carbohydrates, 16g fat, 2g fiber, 0mg cholesterol, 10mg sodium, 320mg potassium.

# Sweet Chili Mango Sauce

## INGREDIENTS

- 2 ripe mangoes, peeled and pitted
- 1/4 cup apple cider vinegar
- 1/4 cup agave syrup or maple syrup
- 2 cloves garlic, minced
- 1 small red chili, finely chopped (adjust for heat preference)
- 1/4 teaspoon ginger powder
- Salt, to taste
- Juice of half a lime

Prep Time: 10 minutes

Cook Time: 15 minutes

Serves: 4

## DIRECTIONS

Combine mangoes, apple cider vinegar, agave syrup, garlic, red chili, and ginger powder in the Instant Pot. Set the Instant Pot to "Sauté" mode and cook for about 10-12 minutes, stirring occasionally, until the mangoes break down and the mixture becomes saucy. Turn off the Instant Pot and let the sauce cool slightly. Transfer the mixture to a blender, add lime juice and salt, and blend until smooth.

## NUTRITIONAL INFORMATION

Per serving: 110 calories, 1g protein, 28g carbohydrates, 0.5g fat, 2g fiber, 0mg cholesterol, 5mg sodium, 180mg potassium.

# Classic Vegan Tzatziki

## INGREDIENTS

- 1 cup unsweetened vegan yogurt (coconut or almond-based work well)
- 1 medium cucumber, finely grated and drained
- 2 cloves garlic, minced
- 1 tablespoon fresh dill, chopped
- 2 tablespoons lemon juice
- 1 tablespoon olive oil
- Salt and pepper, to taste
- 1 tablespoon chopped fresh mint (optional)

Prep Time: 15 min

Cook Time: 0 minutes

Serves: 4

## DIRECTIONS

Begin by grating the cucumber. Place the grated cucumber in a cloth or sieve and squeeze to remove as much liquid as possible. In a mixing bowl, combine the drained cucumber, vegan yogurt, minced garlic, fresh dill, lemon juice, and olive oil. Mix until well combined. Season with salt and pepper, adjusting according to taste. If desired, stir in the fresh mint for an added layer of flavor. Chill before serving for the best flavor. The tzatziki can be stored in an airtight container in the fridge for up to 3 days.

## NUTRITIONAL INFORMATION

Per serving: 80 calories, 2g protein, 8g carbohydrates, 4g fat, 1g fiber, 0mg cholesterol, 20mg sodium, 150mg potassium.

# Lemon Tahini Drizzle

## INGREDIENTS

- 1/2 cup tahini
- 3 tablespoons fresh lemon juice
- 2 cloves garlic, minced
- 2 tablespoons olive oil
- 3-5 tablespoons water (adjust for desired consistency)
- Salt, to taste
- 1 tablespoon chopped fresh parsley (optional)

Prep Time: 10 min

Cook Time: 0 minutes

Serves: 4

## DIRECTIONS

In a mixing bowl, whisk together tahini, lemon juice, minced garlic, and olive oil until smooth. Slowly add water, one tablespoon at a time, whisking continuously until you reach the desired consistency. Season with salt, adjusting according to taste. If desired, fold in the fresh parsley for a hint of freshness. Store in an airtight container in the refrigerator. Stir well before using as the dressing may separate over time.

## NUTRITIONAL INFORMATION

Per serving: 190 calories, 4g protein, 7g carbohydrates, 17g fat, 2g fiber, 0mg cholesterol, 20mg sodium, 100mg potassium.

# Roasted Garlic Hummus

## INGREDIENTS

- 1 whole head of garlic
- 1 tablespoon olive oil
- 1 can (15 oz) chickpeas, drained and rinsed
- 3 tablespoons tahini
- 2 tablespoons fresh lemon juice
- 2 tablespoons water
- 1/4 teaspoon ground cumin
- Salt, to taste
- 2 tablespoons chopped fresh parsley (for garnish, optional)

 Prep Time: 15 min    Cook Time: 40 minutes    Serves: 4

## DIRECTIONS

Cut the top off the garlic head, drizzle with olive oil, wrap in foil, and place in the Instant Pot on the trivet. Add 1 cup of water, seal, and set to 'Manual' or 'Pressure Cook' for 20 minutes. Quick release and let garlic cool. Squeeze cloves into a food processor. Add chickpeas, tahini, lemon juice, water, cumin, and salt. Blend until smooth, scraping down the sides. Adjust seasoning. If too thick, add water, a tablespoon at a time. Transfer to a serving bowl, garnish with parsley, and drizzle with more olive oil before serving.

## NUTRITIONAL INFORMATION

Per serving: 210 calories, 8g protein, 27g carbohydrates, 9g fat, 7g fiber, 0mg cholesterol, 300mg sodium, 220mg potassium.

# Sunflower Seed Pâté

## INGREDIENTS

- 1 cup raw sunflower seeds, soaked for 2-4 hours and drained
- 1/2 cup chopped red bell pepper
- 2 green onions, chopped
- 2 tablespoons lemon juice
- 2 tablespoons nutritional yeast
- 1 clove garlic, minced
- 1/2 teaspoon salt
- 1/4 teaspoon black pepper
- 2 tablespoons fresh chopped parsley
- 1/4 cup water (or more as needed)

 Prep Time: 10 min    Cook Time: 5 minutes    Serves: 4

## DIRECTIONS

In the Instant Pot, combine soaked sunflower seeds with enough water to cover them by an inch. Set the pot to 'Manual' or 'Pressure Cook' on high for 5 minutes. Once done, release the pressure naturally. Drain the sunflower seeds and place them in a food processor. Add the red bell pepper, green onions, lemon juice, nutritional yeast, garlic, salt, pepper, and parsley to the food processor. Blend until smooth, adding water in small amounts as necessary to reach your desired consistency. Adjust seasoning as needed. Transfer to a bowl and refrigerate for an hour before serving to allow flavors to meld.

## NUTRITIONAL INFORMATION

Per serving: 190 calories, 7g protein, 9g carbohydrates, 15g fat, 4g fiber, 0mg cholesterol, 320mg sodium, 250mg potassium.

# Mint Cilantro Chutney

## INGREDIENTS

- 1 cup fresh mint leaves, packed
- 1 cup fresh cilantro leaves, packed
- 2 green chilies, deseeded (adjust to taste)
- 1 inch ginger, chopped
- 1 clove garlic, minced
- 1 tablespoon lemon juice
- 1/2 teaspoon salt (adjust to taste)
- 1/2 teaspoon cumin seeds
- 1/4 cup water (or more for desired consistency)

 Prep Time: 10 min

 Cook Time: 2 minutes

 Serves: 4

## DIRECTIONS

Rinse the mint and cilantro leaves under cold water and pat dry with a kitchen towel. In the Instant Pot on the 'Sauté' setting, dry roast the cumin seeds for about a minute or until aromatic. Turn off the Instant Pot. Add the mint, cilantro, green chilies, ginger, garlic, lemon juice, salt, and water into the pot. Use an immersion blender directly in the pot to blend everything together until smooth, adding water if necessary to reach the desired consistency. Alternatively, you can transfer the ingredients to a blender or food processor to blend. Transfer to a container and refrigerate. Serve chilled.

## NUTRITIONAL INFORMATION

Per serving: 15 calories, 0.5g protein, 3g carbohydrates, 0.2g fat, 1g fiber, 0mg cholesterol, 300mg sodium, 100mg potassium.

Salads &
Slaws

# Crunchy Asian Cabbage Salad

## INGREDIENTS

- 2 cups shredded green cabbage, red cabbage
- 1 carrot, julienned or shredded
- 1 bell pepper, thinly sliced
- 3 green onions, sliced
- 1/4 cup toasted slivered almonds, sesame seeds
- 1/4 cup edamame beans
- 3 tablespoons rice vinegar
- 1 tablespoon soy sauce
- 1 tablespoon maple syrup or agave nectar
- 1 tablespoon toasted sesame oil, grated fresh ginger
- 1 clove garlic, minced
- 1 tablespoon lime juice

Prep Time: 15 min

Cook Time: 0 minutes

Serves: 4

## DIRECTIONS

In a large mixing bowl, combine the green cabbage, red cabbage, carrot, bell pepper, green onions, almonds, sesame seeds, and edamame. In a separate small bowl, whisk together all the dressing ingredients until well combined. Pour the dressing over the salad mixture and toss well to coat. Let the salad sit for about 10 minutes for the flavors to meld, then serve immediately.

## NUTRITIONAL INFORMATION

Per serving: 180 calories, 6g protein, 22g carbohydrates, 9g fat, 5g fiber, 0mg cholesterol, 310mg sodium, 400mg potassium.


# Mediterranean Chickpea Salad

## INGREDIENTS

- 2 cups cooked chickpeas (canned or pre-cooked)
- 1 cup cherry tomatoes, halved
- 1 cucumber, diced
- 1/2 red onion, finely chopped
- 1/4 cup Kalamata olives, pitted and sliced
- 1/4 cup fresh parsley, chopped
- 2 tablespoons fresh lemon juice
- 2 tablespoons extra virgin olive oil
- 1 garlic clove, minced

Prep Time: 10 min

Cook Time: 0 minutes

Serves: 4

## DIRECTIONS

In a large bowl, combine chickpeas, cherry tomatoes, cucumber, red onion, olives, and parsley. In a separate smaller bowl, whisk together the lemon juice, olive oil, minced garlic, salt, and pepper to create the dressing. Pour the dressing over the chickpea mixture and toss well to ensure everything is well coated. Refrigerate for about 30 minutes to let the flavors meld together, then serve.

## NUTRITIONAL INFORMATION

Per serving: 270 calories, 9g protein, 36g carbohydrates, 11g fat, 9g fiber, 0mg cholesterol, 300mg sodium, 470mg potassium.

# Quinoa Tabouli Delight

## INGREDIENTS

- 1 cup quinoa, rinsed and drained
- 2 cups water
- 1 cup fresh parsley, finely chopped
- 1/2 cup fresh mint, finely chopped
- 4 green onions, sliced
- 2 tomatoes, diced
- 1 cucumber, diced
- 1/4 cup extra virgin olive oil
- 3 tablespoons fresh lemon juice
- 1 garlic clove, minced
- Salt and pepper to taste

Prep Time: 15 min      Cook Time: 15 minutes      Serves: 4

## DIRECTIONS

In the Instant Pot, add quinoa and water. Close the lid and set the valve to sealing. Select Manual/Pressure Cook setting at high pressure for 1 minute. Once done, let the pressure release naturally for 10 minutes, then quick release any remaining pressure. Transfer cooked quinoa to a large bowl and let it cool for a few minutes. Add parsley, mint, green onions, tomatoes, and cucumber to the bowl with quinoa. In a separate smaller bowl, whisk together the olive oil, lemon juice, garlic, salt, and pepper. Pour the dressing over the quinoa mixture and toss well to combine.

## NUTRITIONAL INFORMATION

Per serving: 250 calories, 7g protein, 35g carbohydrates, 10g fat, 5g fiber, 0mg cholesterol, 150mg sodium, 400mg potassium.

# Beetroot and Spinach Salad

## INGREDIENTS

- 4 medium-sized beets, peeled and diced
- 1 cup water
- 4 cups fresh spinach, washed and torn
- 1/4 cup red onion, thinly sliced
- 1/4 cup walnuts, roughly chopped
- 2 tablespoons extra virgin olive oil
- 2 tablespoons balsamic vinegar
- 1 tablespoon lemon juice
- Salt and pepper to taste

Prep Time: 10 min      Cook Time: 25 minutes      Serves: 4

## DIRECTIONS

Place the diced beets and water in the Instant Pot. Close the lid and set the valve to sealing. Select Manual/Pressure Cook setting at high pressure for 15 minutes. Once done, quick release the pressure. Drain the beets and let them cool for a few minutes. In a large salad bowl, combine the cooled beets, spinach, red onion, and walnuts. In a small bowl, whisk together the olive oil, balsamic vinegar, lemon juice, salt, and pepper. Pour the dressing over the salad and toss gently to combine.

## NUTRITIONAL INFORMATION

Per serving: 180 calories, 4g protein, 20g carbohydrates, 10g fat, 4g fiber, 0mg cholesterol, 150mg sodium, 500mg potassium.

# Creamy Coleslaw with Apples

## INGREDIENTS

- 3 cups shredded green cabbage
- 1 cup shredded red cabbage
- 2 medium apples, cored and thinly sliced
- 1/2 cup vegan mayonnaise
- 2 tablespoons apple cider vinegar
- 1 tablespoon agave nectar or maple syrup
- Salt and pepper to taste
- 2 tablespoons fresh parsley, chopped (optional)
- 1/4 cup chopped walnuts (optional)

Prep Time: 15 min

Cook Time: 0 minutes

Serves: 4

## DIRECTIONS

In a large bowl, combine the green cabbage, red cabbage, and sliced apples. In a separate smaller bowl, whisk together the vegan mayonnaise, apple cider vinegar, agave nectar or maple syrup, salt, and pepper until smooth. Pour the dressing over the cabbage and apple mixture. Toss until everything is well-coated with the dressing. If desired, garnish with fresh parsley and chopped walnuts before serving.

## NUTRITIONAL INFORMATION

Per serving: 250 calories, 2g protein, 32g carbohydrates, 13g fat, 4g fiber, 0mg cholesterol, 230mg sodium, 300mg potassium.

# Hearty Lentil and Vegetable Salad

## INGREDIENTS

- 1 cup dried green lentils, rinsed and drained
- 2.5 cups vegetable broth
- 1 medium carrot, diced
- 1 bell pepper (color of choice), diced
- 1 small red onion, finely chopped
- 1 cup cherry tomatoes, halved
- 2 tablespoons olive oil
- 2 tablespoons apple cider vinegar
- 1 tablespoon Dijon mustard
- 1 clove garlic, minced
- Salt and pepper to taste
- Fresh herbs (like parsley or cilantro) for garnish, chopped

Prep Time: 15 minutes

Cook Time: 15 minutes

Serves: 4

## DIRECTIONS

Add the lentils and vegetable broth to the Instant Pot. Close the lid and set to Manual/High Pressure for 15 minutes. Once done, quick release the pressure and drain any excess broth. While the lentils are cooking, in a large bowl, combine the diced carrot, bell pepper, red onion, and cherry tomatoes. Prepare the dressing by whisking together the olive oil, apple cider vinegar, Dijon mustard, minced garlic, salt, and pepper in a small bowl. Once the lentils have cooled slightly, add them to the bowl of vegetables. Pour the dressing over the top and toss everything together until well combined. Garnish with fresh herbs before serving.

## NUTRITIONAL INFORMATION

Per serving: 280 calories, 15g protein, 40g carbohydrates, 7g fat, 15g fiber, 0mg cholesterol, 400mg sodium, 600mg potassium.

# Moroccan Carrot Salad

## INGREDIENTS

- 4 cups of carrots, peeled and sliced into thin rounds
- 1 cup of water
- 2 tablespoons olive oil
- 2 cloves garlic, minced
- 1 teaspoon ground cumin
- 1/2 teaspoon ground paprika
- 1/4 teaspoon ground cinnamon
- 2 tablespoons fresh lemon juice
- 1/4 cup chopped fresh cilantro
- 1/4 cup chopped fresh parsley
- 2 tablespoons raisins

 Prep Time: 10 min

 Cook Time: 5 minutes

 Serves: 4

## DIRECTIONS

Place the carrot rounds and water in the Instant Pot. Close the lid and set to Manual/High Pressure for 2 minutes. Quick release the pressure and drain the carrots. In a large mixing bowl, combine olive oil, minced garlic, cumin, paprika, cinnamon, and lemon juice to make the dressing. Toss the steamed carrots in the dressing until well-coated. Allow the salad to cool for a few minutes. Mix in cilantro, parsley, raisins, and roasted almonds. Season with salt and pepper to taste. Serve chilled or at room temperature.

## NUTRITIONAL INFORMATION

Per serving: 150 calories, 2g protein, 20g carbohydrates, 8g fat, 4g fiber, 0mg cholesterol, 80mg sodium, 450mg potassium.

# Cilantro Lime Corn Salad

## INGREDIENTS

- 4 cups of corn kernels (fresh or frozen)
- 1 cup of cherry tomatoes, halved
- 1/4 cup finely chopped red onion
- 1/4 cup chopped fresh cilantro
- 2 limes, zested and juiced
- 1 tablespoon olive oil
- 1 jalapeño, seeds removed and finely chopped (optional for added heat)
- Salt and pepper to taste
- 1 avocado, diced (optional for added creaminess)

 Prep Time: 15 min

 Cook Time: 5 minutes

 Serves: 4

## DIRECTIONS

Pour 1 cup of water into the Instant Pot. Place the trivet or steaming basket inside and add the corn kernels on top. Set to Manual/High Pressure for 2 minutes. Quick release the pressure and transfer corn to a mixing bowl. Add cherry tomatoes, red onion, cilantro, lime zest, lime juice, olive oil, and jalapeño (if using) to the bowl with corn. Toss to combine. Season the salad with salt and pepper according to taste. If using, gently fold in the diced avocado. Allow the salad to sit for a few minutes, enabling the flavors to meld. Serve either chilled or at room temperature.

## NUTRITIONAL INFORMATION

Per serving: 180 calories, 4g protein, 35g carbohydrates, 6g fat, 5g fiber, 0mg cholesterol, 25mg sodium, 400mg potassium.

# Mediterranean Orzo Salad

## INGREDIENTS

- 1 cup orzo pasta (uncooked)
- 2 1/2 cups water (for cooking orzo)
- 1 cup cherry tomatoes, halved
- 1/2 cup chopped cucumber
- 1/2 cup Kalamata olives, pitted and sliced
- 1/4 cup finely chopped red onion
- 1/4 cup chopped fresh parsley
- 1/4 cup extra-virgin olive oil
- 2 tablespoons fresh lemon juice
- 1 garlic clove, minced

Prep Time: 15 min     Cook Time: 5 minutes     Serves: 4

## DIRECTIONS

Pour the water into the Instant Pot and add the orzo. Set the Instant Pot to Manual/High Pressure for 3 minutes. Once the cooking cycle is complete, do a quick release of the pressure. Drain any excess water from the orzo and transfer it to a mixing bowl. Add the cherry tomatoes, cucumber, Kalamata olives, red onion, and parsley to the bowl with orzo. In a separate smaller bowl, whisk together olive oil, lemon juice, minced garlic, salt, and pepper. Pour this dressing over the orzo mixture and toss well to combine. If desired, gently fold in the vegan feta cheese. Chill the salad for about an hour before serving for best flavor.

## NUTRITIONAL INFORMATION

Per serving: 310 calories, 8g protein, 40g carbohydrates, 15g fat, 3g fiber, 0mg cholesterol, 300mg sodium, 200mg potassium.

# Spicy Kale and Avocado Slaw

## INGREDIENTS

- 4 cups kale, stems removed and finely chopped
- 2 ripe avocados, pitted, peeled, and diced
- 1 red bell pepper, finely sliced
- 1/4 cup fresh cilantro, chopped
- 2 green onions, finely sliced
- 1 jalapeño, seeded and finely diced (adjust according to spice preference)
- Juice of 1 lime
- 2 tablespoons olive oil
- 1 tablespoon apple cider vinegar

Prep Time: 15 min     Cook Time: 1 minute     Serves: 4

## DIRECTIONS

Add 1 cup of water to the Instant Pot. Place the kale in a steamer basket or on a trivet inside the pot. Set the Instant Pot to Steam mode for 1 minute. Once complete, do a quick release of the pressure and remove the kale. Let it cool for a few minutes. In a large mixing bowl, combine the steamed kale, avocado, red bell pepper, cilantro, green onions, and jalapeño. In a smaller bowl, whisk together the lime juice, olive oil, apple cider vinegar, salt, pepper, and red pepper flakes, if using. Pour the dressing over the kale mixture and toss gently until everything is well coated. Serve immediately or refrigerate for an hour to allow flavors to meld.

## NUTRITIONAL INFORMATION

Per serving: 220 calories, 4g protein, 20g carbohydrates, 15g fat, 7g fiber, 0mg cholesterol, 150mg sodium, 650mg potassium.

# Citrus Fennel Salad

## INGREDIENTS

- 2 medium fennel bulbs, thinly sliced
- 2 oranges, peeled and segmented
- 1 grapefruit, peeled and segmented
- 1 lemon, zest and juice
- 2 tablespoons olive oil
- 1 tablespoon maple syrup or agave nectar
- Salt and pepper to taste
- 1/4 cup fresh mint leaves, chopped
- 1/4 cup pomegranate seeds (optional for added crunch and color)

 Prep Time: 15 min

 Cook Time: 0 minutes

 Serves: 4

## DIRECTIONS

In a large salad bowl, combine the thinly sliced fennel, orange segments, and grapefruit segments. In a separate small bowl, whisk together lemon zest, lemon juice, olive oil, maple syrup or agave nectar, salt, and pepper to create the dressing. Pour the dressing over the fennel and citrus mixture, tossing gently to coat. Garnish the salad with chopped mint and optional pomegranate seeds before serving.

## NUTRITIONAL INFORMATION

Per serving: 160 calories, 2g protein, 25g carbohydrates, 7g fat, 6g fiber, 0mg cholesterol, 80mg sodium, 500mg potassium.

# BBQ Jackfruit Salad

## INGREDIENTS

- 2 cans (20 oz each) young green jackfruit in water, drained and rinsed
- 1 cup BBQ sauce (plant-based, no added sugars)
- 1 cup vegetable broth
- 1 red bell pepper, thinly sliced
- 1 green bell pepper, thinly sliced
- 1 small red onion, thinly sliced
- 4 cups mixed salad greens (e.g., arugula, spinach, romaine)
- 1/2 cup cherry tomatoes, halved
- 1/4 cup fresh cilantro, chopped
- Salt and pepper to taste

 Prep Time: 15 min

 Cook Time: 30 minutes

 Serves: 4

## DIRECTIONS

Using your hands, shred the jackfruit into pieces resembling pulled meat. Place it into the Instant Pot. Add BBQ sauce, vegetable broth, red bell pepper, green bell pepper, and red onion to the Instant Pot. Stir well to mix. Seal the Instant Pot and set it to 'Manual' or 'Pressure Cook' mode for 15 minutes. Once done, release pressure naturally. As the jackfruit is cooling slightly, arrange the salad greens on plates. Top with cherry tomatoes. Spoon the BBQ jackfruit mixture over the greens. Garnish with fresh cilantro, season with salt and pepper if needed, and serve immediately.

## NUTRITIONAL INFORMATION

Per serving: 250 calories, 3g protein, 58g carbohydrates, 1g fat, 8g fiber, 0mg cholesterol, 450mg sodium, 650mg potassium.

# Waldorf-inspired Salad

## INGREDIENTS

- 2 red apples, cored and chopped
- 1 cup seedless red grapes, halved
- 1/2 cup celery, chopped
- 1/2 cup walnut pieces
- 1/2 cup raisins
- 1 cup water
- 1/4 cup plant-based mayonnaise
- 1 tsp lemon juice
- Salt and pepper to taste
- Mixed salad greens for serving

Prep Time: 10 min          Cook Time: 4 minutes          Serves: 4

## DIRECTIONS

In the Instant Pot, combine chopped apples, grapes, celery, walnuts, raisins, and water. Secure the lid and set the Instant Pot to 'Manual' or 'Pressure Cook' mode for 4 minutes. Once done, quick release the pressure and drain any excess water. Transfer the fruit and nut mixture to a large bowl and let it cool for a few minutes. In a separate small bowl, whisk together plant-based mayonnaise, lemon juice, salt, and pepper. Pour this dressing over the fruit and nut mixture, and toss to combine. Serve the Waldorf-inspired salad over mixed greens.

## NUTRITIONAL INFORMATION

Per serving: 260 calories, 4g protein, 36g carbohydrates, 12g fat, 4g fiber, 0mg cholesterol, 160mg sodium, 400mg potassium.

# Sesame Ginger Noodle Salad

## INGREDIENTS

- 8 oz rice noodles or whole grain spaghetti
- 2 cups snap peas, trimmed
- 1 red bell pepper, thinly sliced
- 2 carrots, julienned
- 3 green onions, chopped
- 2 tablespoons sesame seeds
- 1/4 cup low-sodium soy sauce or tamari
- 1 tablespoon rice vinegar
- 2 teaspoons fresh ginger, grated
- 2 garlic cloves, minced
- 1 tablespoon agave nectar or maple syrup

Prep Time: 15 min          Cook Time: 5 minutes          Serves: 4

## DIRECTIONS

In the Instant Pot, add rice noodles and enough water to cover them. Secure the lid and set the Instant Pot to 'Manual' or 'Pressure Cook' mode for 5 minutes. Once done, quick release the pressure and drain the noodles. Transfer them to a large mixing bowl. To the bowl with noodles, add snap peas, bell pepper, carrots, green onions, and cilantro. In a separate bowl, whisk together all the dressing ingredients until well combined. Pour the dressing over the noodle and vegetable mixture. Toss everything together to ensure the ingredients are evenly coated. Sprinkle sesame seeds on top, toss again lightly, and serve.

## NUTRITIONAL INFORMATION

Per serving: 320 calories, 7g protein, 54g carbohydrates, 10g fat, 4g fiber, 0mg cholesterol, 600mg sodium, 350mg potassium.

# Avocado and Toasted Pecan Salad

## INGREDIENTS

- 2 large avocados, diced
- 1 cup pecans
- 4 cups mixed salad greens (e.g., arugula, spinach, romaine)
- 1/2 red onion, thinly sliced
- 1/4 cup dried cranberries
- 1 tablespoon olive oil
- 3 tablespoons fresh lemon juice
- 1/4 cup olive oil
- 1 teaspoon agave nectar or maple syrup
- Salt and pepper to taste

Prep Time: 10 min

Cook Time: 5 minutes

Serves: 4

## DIRECTIONS

Turn the Instant Pot on 'Sauté' mode and add 1 tablespoon of olive oil. Once heated, add the pecans and toast for 2-3 minutes, stirring frequently, until they are slightly browned and fragrant. Transfer to a plate and let cool. In a large salad bowl, combine the mixed greens, red onion, avocado, toasted pecans, and dried cranberries. In a small bowl, whisk together the ingredients for the lemon vinaigrette dressing. Drizzle the dressing over the salad mixture and gently toss until all ingredients are well coated. Serve immediately.

## NUTRITIONAL INFORMATION

Per serving: 370 calories, 5g protein, 20g carbohydrates, 31g fat, 8g fiber, 0mg cholesterol, 20mg sodium, 600mg potassium.

Delightful
Desserts

# Pressure-Cooked Berry Compote

## INGREDIENTS

- 2 cups fresh strawberries, hulled and halved
- 1 cup fresh blueberries
- 1 cup fresh raspberries
- 1/4 cup agave nectar or maple syrup
- 1 teaspoon lemon zest
- 2 tablespoons lemon juice
- 1 teaspoon vanilla extract

Prep Time: 5 min

Cook Time: 10 minutes

Serves: 4

## DIRECTIONS

In the Instant Pot, combine strawberries, blueberries, raspberries, agave nectar (or maple syrup), lemon zest, and lemon juice. Lock the lid in place and select the "Manual" setting. Adjust the pressure to "High" and set the time for 5 minutes. Once the cooking time is up, allow the Instant Pot to release pressure naturally for 5 minutes. After that, quick release any remaining pressure. Stir in the vanilla extract, then transfer the compote to a bowl and let it cool. The mixture will thicken as it cools. Serve over oatmeal, yogurt, pancakes, or enjoy it on its own.

## NUTRITIONAL INFORMATION

Per serving: 110 calories, 1g protein, 28g carbohydrates, 0.5g fat, 4g fiber, 0mg cholesterol, 5mg sodium, 200mg potassium..

# Vegan Chocolate Lava Cake

## INGREDIENTS

- 1 cup all-purpose flour
- 1/4 cup unsweetened cocoa powder
- 1/2 teaspoon baking powder
- 1/4 teaspoon salt
- 1/2 cup coconut sugar or brown sugar
- 1/3 cup unsweetened almond milk (or any plant-based milk)
- 1/4 cup coconut oil, melted
- 1 teaspoon vanilla extract
- 1/2 cup vegan dark chocolate chunks or chips
- 1/2 cup hot water

Prep Time: 15 min

Cook Time: 9 minutes

Serves: 4

## DIRECTIONS

In a mixing bowl, sift together flour, cocoa powder, baking powder, and salt. Stir in the coconut sugar. Pour in the almond milk, melted coconut oil, and vanilla extract. Mix until well combined. Divide the batter among four ramekins. Press several chocolate chunks or chips into the center of each. Place a trivet inside the Instant Pot and pour in 1 cup of water. Place the ramekins on the trivet. Lock the lid and set the Instant Pot to "Manual" mode, high pressure, for 9 minutes. Once done, do a quick pressure release. Carefully remove the ramekins, let them cool slightly, and then serve while still warm.

## NUTRITIONAL INFORMATION

Per serving: 320 calories, 4g protein, 52g carbohydrates, 13g fat, 4g fiber, 0mg cholesterol, 80mg sodium, 180mg potassium.

# Instant Pot Rice Pudding

## INGREDIENTS

- 1 cup Arborio rice
- 2 cups almond milk (or any plant-based milk of choice)
- 1/4 cup coconut sugar or maple syrup
- 1/4 teaspoon salt
- 1 teaspoon vanilla extract
- 1/2 teaspoon ground cinnamon (optional)
- 1/4 cup raisins or dried fruit of choice (optional)
- Zest of 1 lemon or orange (optional)

Prep Time: 10 min

Cook Time: 25 minutes

Serves: 4

5

## DIRECTIONS

Rinse the Arborio rice under cold water until the water runs clear. In the Instant Pot, combine the rinsed rice, almond milk, coconut sugar or maple syrup, and salt. Lock the lid and set the Instant Pot to "Manual" or "Pressure Cook" mode, low pressure, for 20 minutes. Once done, allow a natural pressure release for 5 minutes, then release the remaining pressure manually. Open the lid, stir in the vanilla extract, cinnamon, raisins, and zest (if using). Let the pudding sit for a few minutes to thicken.

## NUTRITIONAL INFORMATION

Per serving: 220 calories, 3g protein, 48g carbohydrates, 2g fat, 1g fiber, 0mg cholesterol, 80mg sodium, 100mg potassium.

# Caramelized Banana Delight

## INGREDIENTS

- 4 ripe bananas, sliced into half-inch pieces
- 2 tablespoons coconut oil
- 3 tablespoons maple syrup or agave nectar
- 1/2 teaspoon ground cinnamon
- Pinch of salt
- 1 teaspoon vanilla extract
- Optional toppings: toasted coconut flakes, chopped nuts, vegan whipped cream, or vegan ice cream

Prep Time: 5 minutes

Cook Time: 10 minutes

Serves: 4

## DIRECTIONS

Turn the Instant Pot to "Sauté" mode and add the coconut oil, allowing it to melt. Once hot, add the banana slices, maple syrup or agave nectar, cinnamon, and salt. Sauté until the bananas are golden and caramelized, stirring occasionally for about 5 minutes. Turn off the Instant Pot, stir in the vanilla extract, and let the mixture sit for 1-2 minutes. Serve hot, topped with your choice of optional toppings if desired.

## NUTRITIONAL INFORMATION

Per serving: 210 calories, 1g protein, 45g carbohydrates, 5g fat, 3g fiber, 0mg cholesterol, 20mg sodium, 450mg potassium.

# Coconut Mango Sticky Rice

## INGREDIENTS

- 1 cup glutinous (sticky) rice, rinsed and drained
- 1 1/4 cups water
- 1 can (13.5 oz) full-fat coconut milk
- 1/2 cup coconut sugar or agave nectar
- 1/2 teaspoon salt
- 2 ripe mangoes, peeled, pitted, and sliced
- Toasted sesame seeds or mung beans for garnish (optional)
- 1 teaspoon cornstarch (mixed with 2 tablespoons water) to thicken the sauce if needed

 Prep Time: 10 min

 Cook Time: 20 minutes

 Serves: 4

## DIRECTIONS

Add the rinsed rice and water to the Instant Pot. Secure the lid, set the valve to "Sealing", and select the "Rice" setting or manually set to cook on high pressure for 12 minutes. Once the rice is cooked, allow the pressure to naturally release for 10 minutes, then quick release any remaining pressure. Fluff the rice with a fork. In a separate saucepan, combine the coconut milk, coconut sugar or agave nectar, and salt. Heat over medium heat, stirring until the sugar is dissolved. If you want a thicker sauce, add the cornstarch mixture and stir until it thickens. Serve the sticky rice in bowls topped with mango slices. Drizzle the warm coconut sauce over the top and garnish with toasted sesame seeds or mung beans if desired.

## NUTRITIONAL INFORMATION

Per serving: 380 calories, 5g protein, 74g carbohydrates, 9g fat, 3g fiber, 0mg cholesterol, 150mg sodium, 450mg potassium.

# Spiced Apple Crumble

## INGREDIENTS

- 5 large apples, peeled, cored, and sliced
- 1/4 cup maple syrup or agave nectar
- 1 teaspoon ground cinnamon
- 1/2 teaspoon ground nutmeg
- 1/4 cup water
- 3/4 cup rolled oats
- 1/3 cup almond flour
- 1/4 cup coconut sugar or brown sugar
- 1/2 teaspoon ground cinnamon
- 1/4 cup coconut oil, melted
- A pinch of salt

 Prep Time: 15 min

 Cook Time: 8 minutes

 Serves: 4

## DIRECTIONS

In the Instant Pot, combine sliced apples, maple syrup or agave nectar, cinnamon, nutmeg, and water. Stir to coat the apples evenly. In a separate mixing bowl, combine the rolled oats, almond flour, coconut sugar, cinnamon, melted coconut oil, and a pinch of salt. Mix until the ingredients are well-combined and a crumbly texture forms. Evenly spread the crumble topping over the apples in the Instant Pot. Secure the Instant Pot lid, set the valve to "Sealing", and select the "Manual" setting. Adjust the time to 8 minutes on high pressure. Once done, quick release the pressure.

## NUTRITIONAL INFORMATION

Per serving: 410 calories, 4g protein, 65g carbohydrates, 17g fat, 7g fiber, 0mg cholesterol, 10mg sodium, 350mg potassium.

# Creamy Vegan Cheesecake

## INGREDIENTS

- 1 cup vegan graham cracker crumbs (or similar)
- 1/4 cup melted coconut oil
- 2 tablespoons coconut sugar or maple syrup
- 1 1/2 cups raw cashews, soaked overnight and drained
- 3/4 cup canned full-fat coconut milk
- 2/3 cup maple syrup or agave nectar
- 1/4 cup coconut oil, melted
- 2 tablespoons fresh lemon juice
- 2 teaspoons vanilla extract

 Prep Time: 15 min

 Cook Time: 30 minutes

 Serves: 4

## DIRECTIONS

Combine graham cracker crumbs, melted coconut oil, and coconut sugar or maple syrup in a mixing bowl. Press this mixture into the bottom of a springform pan that fits your Instant Pot. In a high-speed blender, blend soaked cashews, coconut milk, maple syrup or agave nectar, melted coconut oil, lemon juice, vanilla extract, and salt until the mixture is silky smooth. Pour the filling mixture over the crust in the springform pan. Add 1 cup of water to the bottom of the Instant Pot. Place the springform pan on the trivet and lower it into the Instant Pot. Seal the lid and set the pot to "Manual" mode for 30 minutes on high pressure. Once done, allow a natural pressure release for 10 minutes, then carefully release any remaining pressure. Remove cheesecake, let it cool, then refrigerate for at least 4 hours, preferably overnight.

## NUTRITIONAL INFORMATION

Per serving: 580 calories, 8g protein, 50g carbohydrates, 40g fat, 2g fiber, 0mg cholesterol, 180mg sodium, 320mg potassium.

# Chocolate Quinoa Pudding

## INGREDIENTS

- 1 cup quinoa, rinsed and drained
- 2 cups almond milk or any plant-based milk of choice
- 1/4 cup cocoa powder
- 1/3 cup maple syrup or agave nectar
- 1 teaspoon vanilla extract
- A pinch of salt

 Prep Time: 10 min

 Cook Time: 15 minutes

 Serves: 4

## DIRECTIONS

In the Instant Pot, combine quinoa, almond milk, cocoa powder, maple syrup or agave nectar, vanilla extract, and a pinch of salt. Seal the lid and set the pot to "Manual" or "Pressure Cook" mode for 15 minutes on high pressure. Once done, allow a natural pressure release for 10 minutes, then carefully release any remaining pressure. Stir the pudding well. It will continue to thicken as it cools. Serve warm or refrigerate and serve cold. Add optional toppings if desired.

## NUTRITIONAL INFORMATION

Per serving: 270 calories, 8g protein, 50g carbohydrates, 5g fat, 5g fiber, 0mg cholesterol, 80mg sodium, 320mg potassium.

# Pumpkin Spice Custard

## INGREDIENTS

- 2 cups pumpkin puree
- 1 can (13.5 oz) full-fat coconut milk
- 1/2 cup maple syrup or agave nectar
- 2 tablespoons cornstarch or arrowroot powder
- 2 teaspoons pumpkin pie spice
- 1 teaspoon vanilla extract
- A pinch of salt

 Prep Time: 15 min

 Cook Time: 25 minutes

 Serves:4

## DIRECTIONS

Whisk together pumpkin puree, coconut milk, maple syrup, cornstarch, pumpkin pie spice, vanilla, and a pinch of salt. Pour into Instant Pot-friendly ramekins. Add 1 cup of water to the Instant Pot with a trivet. Arrange ramekins on the trivet. Close the lid, set to "Manual" or "Pressure Cook" for 10 minutes on high pressure. After cooking, allow a 15-minute natural pressure release, then release any remaining pressure. Carefully remove ramekins. Cool to room temperature, then refrigerate for at least 3 hours or overnight until set.

## NUTRITIONAL INFORMATION

Per serving: 320 calories, 3g protein, 50g carbohydrates, 12g fat, 4g fiber, 0mg cholesterol, 45mg sodium, 350mg potassium.

# Sweetened Red Bean Paste

## INGREDIENTS

- 1 cup adzuki beans (red beans), washed and soaked for 4 hours or overnight
- 3 cups water
- 3/4 cup sugar (adjust to taste)
- 1 pinch of salt

 Prep Time: 10 min

 Cook Time: 40 minutes

 Serves: 4

## DIRECTIONS

Drain the soaked adzuki beans and place them into the Instant Pot. Add 3 cups of water. Seal the Instant Pot lid and set the mode to "Pressure Cook" or "Manual" on high for 20 minutes. After the timer goes off, allow a natural release. Once depressurized, open the lid and drain any excess water. Mash the beans using a masher or immersion blender until smooth. Set the Instant Pot to "Sauté" mode. Stir in the sugar and salt. Continue stirring until the bean paste thickens and achieves a smooth consistency, about 10-15 minutes. Turn off the pot and allow the bean paste to cool.

## NUTRITIONAL INFORMATION

Per serving: 240 calories, 7g protein, 55g carbohydrates, 0.2g fat, 6g fiber, 0mg cholesterol, 60mg sodium, 400mg potassium.

# Pear and Cranberry Compote

## INGREDIENTS

- 4 ripe pears, peeled, cored, and diced
- 1 cup fresh cranberries
- 1/2 cup sugar or maple syrup (adjust to taste)
- 1/2 cup water
- 1 tsp vanilla extract
- 1/2 tsp ground cinnamon
- Zest and juice of 1 lemon

 Prep Time: 10 min

 Cook Time: 7 minutes

 Serves: 4

## DIRECTIONS

In the Instant Pot, combine the diced pears, cranberries, sugar (or maple syrup), water, vanilla extract, cinnamon, lemon zest, and lemon juice. Seal the Instant Pot lid and set the mode to "Pressure Cook" or "Manual" on high for 5 minutes. Once the cooking cycle completes, carefully do a quick release to vent the steam. Open the lid and set the Instant Pot to "Sauté" mode. Allow the compote to simmer, stirring occasionally, until it reaches your desired consistency, approximately 2 minutes.

## NUTRITIONAL INFORMATION

Per serving: 180 calories, 0.5g protein, 45g carbohydrates, 0.3g fat, 5g fiber, 0mg cholesterol, 5mg sodium, 210mg potassium.

# Blueberry Lemon Cake

## INGREDIENTS

- 1 cup all-purpose flour
- 1/2 cup almond flour
- 1 tsp baking powder
- 1/2 tsp baking soda
- 1/4 tsp salt
- 3/4 cup almond milk
- 1/3 cup maple syrup or agave nectar
- 1/4 cup coconut oil, melted
- Zest and juice of 1 lemon
- 1 tsp vanilla extract
- 1 cup fresh blueberries

 Prep Time: 15 minutes

 Cook Time: 40 minutes

 Serves: 4

## DIRECTIONS

In a mixing bowl, whisk together the all-purpose flour, almond flour, baking powder, baking soda, and salt. In another bowl, combine the almond milk, maple syrup, melted coconut oil, lemon zest, lemon juice, and vanilla extract. Mix the wet ingredients into the dry until just combined. Gently fold in the blueberries. Pour the batter into a greased 7-inch springform pan that fits inside your Instant Pot. Cover the pan with aluminum foil. Add 1 cup of water to the Instant Pot. Place the trivet inside, then carefully lower the pan onto the trivet. Seal the lid and set the mode to "Pressure Cook" or "Manual" on high for 40 minutes. Once the cooking cycle completes, let the pressure release naturally for 10 minutes, then do a quick release. Carefully remove the cake, let it cool before serving.

## NUTRITIONAL INFORMATION

Per serving: 375 calories, 6g protein, 45g carbohydrates, 20g fat, 4g fiber, 0mg cholesterol, 300mg sodium, 80mg potassium.

# Chocolate Hazelnut Brownies

## INGREDIENTS

- 1/2 cup hazelnut meal (finely ground hazelnuts)
- 1/4 cup unsweetened cocoa powder
- 1/2 cup coconut sugar or maple syrup
- 1/4 cup melted coconut oil
- 1/4 cup almond milk
- 1 tsp vanilla extract
- 1/2 tsp baking powder
- 1/4 tsp salt
- 1/3 cup vegan chocolate chips
- 1/3 cup chopped hazelnuts for topping

Prep Time: 20 min

Cook Time: 35 minutes

Serves: 4

## DIRECTIONS

Combine hazelnut meal, cocoa powder, baking powder, and salt in a mixing bowl. In another bowl, whisk coconut sugar, melted coconut oil, almond milk, and vanilla extract. Blend wet ingredients into the dry mixture for a thick batter. Fold in chocolate chips. Transfer batter to a greased 7-inch round cake pan or silicone mold. Sprinkle chopped hazelnuts on top. Pour 1 cup of water into the Instant Pot, place the trivet inside, and lower the pan onto the trivet. Secure the lid, set the vent to "Sealing," and pressure cook on high for 35 minutes. After cooking, allow a 10-minute natural pressure release, then quick release. Remove brownies and let them cool before slicing.

## NUTRITIONAL INFORMATION

Per serving: 410 calories, 6g protein, 42g carbohydrates, 27g fat, 5g fiber, 0mg cholesterol, 190mg sodium, 220mg potassium.

# Tapioca Berry Parfait

## INGREDIENTS

- 1/2 cup small pearl tapioca
- 2 1/2 cups almond milk or coconut milk
- 1/4 cup maple syrup or agave nectar
- 1 tsp vanilla extract
- Pinch of salt
- 2 cups mixed berries (strawberries, blueberries, raspberries, and blackberries)
- 1/4 cup chia seeds (for an added texture and nutrition boost)
- 1 cup vegan yogurt (like almond or coconut yogurt)

Prep Time: 10 min

Cook Time: 20 minutes

Serves: 4

## DIRECTIONS

Rinse tapioca pearls under cold water for a couple of minutes. In the Instant Pot, combine tapioca pearls, almond milk, maple syrup, vanilla extract, and a pinch of salt. Stir well. Lock the lid in place and set the Instant Pot to Manual/Pressure Cook on High for 10 minutes. Once done, allow a natural pressure release for 10 minutes, then release the remaining pressure. Let the tapioca cool for a bit. Once cooled, in serving glasses, layer tapioca pudding, chia seeds, vegan yogurt, and mixed berries. Repeat layers until the glasses are filled. Garnish with fresh mint leaves if desired and serve chilled.

## NUTRITIONAL INFORMATION

Per serving: 280 calories, 5g protein, 55g carbohydrates, 6g fat, 7g fiber, 0mg cholesterol, 85mg sodium, 250mg potassium.

# Pecan and Date Tart

## INGREDIENTS

- 1 cup raw pecans, plus extra for garnish
- 1 cup pitted Medjool dates
- 1/2 cup rolled oats
- 1/4 cup coconut oil, melted
- 1/4 teaspoon salt
- 1/2 teaspoon vanilla extract
- 2 tablespoons maple syrup
- 1/4 cup almond milk (or any plant-based milk)
- 1/2 teaspoon ground cinnamon
- Pinch of nutmeg

Prep Time: 15 min

Cook Time: 35 minutes

Serves: 4

## DIRECTIONS

To make the crust, in a food processor, combine dates, rolled oats, 1/4 cup pecans, 2 tablespoons coconut oil, and a pinch of salt. Process until a sticky dough forms. Press the dough into a silicone or non-stick tart pan that can fit inside the Instant Pot. For the filling, blend 3/4 cup of pecans, almond milk, maple syrup, remaining coconut oil, vanilla extract, cinnamon, and nutmeg until smooth. Pour the filling over the crust and spread evenly. Top with extra pecans for garnish. Add 1 cup of water to the Instant Pot. Place the tart pan on the trivet and lower it into the pot. Lock the lid in place and set the Instant Pot to Manual/Pressure Cook on High for 25 minutes. Allow natural pressure release for 10 minutes, then release the remaining pressure. Cool before serving.

## NUTRITIONAL INFORMATION

Per serving: 420 calories, 4g protein, 50g carbohydrates, 25g fat, 6g fiber, 0mg cholesterol, 75mg sodium, 380mg potassium.

Snacks &
Quick Bites

# Instant Pot Vegetable Dumplings

## INGREDIENTS

- 1 cup shredded cabbage
- 1/2 cup finely chopped carrot
- 1/2 cup finely chopped bell pepper
- 1/4 cup finely chopped green onions
- 2 cloves garlic, minced
- 1 tablespoon soy sauce (low-sodium)
- 1 tablespoon sesame oil
- 1/4 teaspoon black pepper
- 1/4 teaspoon ground ginger
- 16 vegan dumpling wrappers
- 1 cup vegetable broth
- Dipping sauce of choice (optional)

Prep Time: 20 min          Cook Time: 15 minutes          Serves: 4

## DIRECTIONS

In a large bowl, mix cabbage, carrot, bell pepper, green onions, garlic, soy sauce, sesame oil, black pepper, and ground ginger. Spoon vegetable mixture onto dumpling wrappers, moisten edges, fold, and seal. In Instant Pot's Sauté mode, heat olive oil and lightly brown dumplings on both sides. Add vegetable broth, ensuring dumplings aren't fully submerged. Close the lid, set Instant Pot to Steam mode, and cook for 5 minutes. After a 5-minute natural pressure release, release remaining pressure. Serve hot with your preferred dipping sauce.

## NUTRITIONAL INFORMATION

Per serving: 210 calories, 5g protein, 35g carbohydrates, 6g fat, 3g fiber, 0mg cholesterol, 320mg sodium, 280mg potassium.

# Spiced Chickpea Popcorn

## INGREDIENTS

- 2 cups cooked chickpeas (rinsed and drained if from a can)
- 1 tablespoon olive oil
- 1/2 teaspoon smoked paprika
- 1/2 teaspoon ground cumin
- 1/4 teaspoon chili powder
- 1/4 teaspoon garlic powder
- 1/4 teaspoon onion powder
- Salt to taste
- Freshly ground black pepper to taste

Prep Time: 10 minutes          Cook Time: 15 minutes          Serves: 4

## DIRECTIONS

Ensure chickpeas are completely dry by patting them down with a kitchen towel. Turn the Instant Pot on Sauté mode and add the olive oil. Once the oil is hot, add chickpeas and all spices. Stir well to ensure chickpeas are evenly coated. Sauté the chickpeas, stirring occasionally, for 10-15 minutes or until they're golden and crispy. Turn off the Instant Pot, transfer chickpeas to a serving bowl, and allow them to cool for a few minutes before serving. They will become crunchier as they cool.

## NUTRITIONAL INFORMATION

Per serving: 130 calories, 6g protein, 18g carbohydrates, 4g fat, 5g fiber, 0mg cholesterol, 200mg sodium, 240mg potassium.

# BBQ Jackfruit Sliders

## INGREDIENTS

- 2 cans (20 oz each) young green jackfruit in water, drained and rinsed
- 1 cup BBQ sauce (ensure it's plant-based)
- 1/2 cup water or vegetable broth
- 1 onion, thinly sliced
- 2 cloves garlic, minced
- 1 tablespoon olive oil
- 1 teaspoon smoked paprika
- Salt and pepper to taste
- 6 plant-based slider buns
- Optional toppings: pickles, coleslaw, vegan mayo

 Prep Time: 15 minutes

 Cook Time: 25 minutes

 Serves: 6

## DIRECTIONS

Set the Instant Pot to Sauté mode. Add olive oil, onions, and garlic. Sauté until onions are translucent. Add drained jackfruit to the Instant Pot, breaking it apart slightly. Add smoked paprika, salt, and pepper. Mix well. Pour in BBQ sauce and water or vegetable broth. Stir until the jackfruit is well-coated. Close the Instant Pot lid, set it to Manual or Pressure Cook on high pressure for 15 minutes. Once done, use the Quick Release method to release the pressure. Once depressurized, open the lid and stir. Use two forks to pull apart the jackfruit until it resembles pulled pork. Serve on slider buns with optional toppings.

## NUTRITIONAL INFORMATION

Per serving: 220 calories, 4g protein, 45g carbohydrates, 3g fat, 5g fiber, 0mg cholesterol, 680mg sodium, 300mg potassium.

# Vegan Spring Rolls with Instant Pot Sauce

## INGREDIENTS

- 12 rice paper wrappers
- 2 cups mixed salad greens
- 1 red bell pepper, thinly sliced
- 1 cucumber, julienned
- 2 carrots, julienned
- 1 avocado, sliced
- 1/2 cup soy sauce
- 1/4 cup rice vinegar
- 2 tablespoons maple syrup or agave
- 1 clove garlic, minced
- 1 teaspoon ginger, minced
- 1/2 teaspoon chili flakes
- 1 cup water

 Prep Time: 20 min

 Cook Time: 10 minutes

 Serves: 6

## DIRECTIONS

Prepare the vegetables, tofu, and herbs, and set aside. To make the sauce, add all the ingredients to the Instant Pot. Set it to Sauté mode and bring the mixture to a simmer. Once simmering, turn off the Instant Pot and let the sauce cool down. This sauce will thicken slightly upon cooling. To assemble the spring rolls, dip a rice paper wrapper into warm water until it becomes soft. Lay it flat on a clean surface. Place a handful of salad greens in the center, followed by a few slices of bell pepper, cucumber, carrots, avocado, and tofu (if using). Add mint and cilantro leaves if desired. Roll up the wrapper, tucking in the sides as you go, similar to a burrito. Repeat with the remaining ingredients.

## NUTRITIONAL INFORMATION

Per serving: 220 calories, 8g protein, 35g carbohydrates, 6g fat, 5g fiber, 0mg cholesterol, 1100mg sodium, 400mg potassium.

# Mushroom and Spinach Potstickers

## INGREDIENTS

- 24 vegan potsticker wrappers
- 1 cup shiitake mushrooms, finely chopped
- 1 cup white button mushrooms, finely chopped
- 2 cups fresh spinach, roughly chopped
- 1 medium onion, finely chopped
- 3 garlic cloves, minced
- 2 tablespoons soy sauce
- 1 tablespoon toasted sesame oil
- 1 teaspoon ginger, grated
- 1/4 cup vegetable broth or water, for steaming

 Prep Time: 30 min

 Cook Time: 20 minutes

 Serves: 6

## DIRECTIONS

Sauté onions, garlic, mushrooms, spinach, ginger, and soy sauce in Instant Pot.

Let mixture cool, then fill potsticker wrappers with a tablespoon of filling. Seal edges, clean Instant Pot, add oil, and brown potstickers for 1-2 minutes. Pour in broth, close lid, pressure cook for 5 mins, then quick release. Serve warm with your favourite dipping sauce.

## NUTRITIONAL INFORMATION

Per serving: 230 calories, 6g protein, 40g carbohydrates, 5g fat, 3g fiber, 0mg cholesterol, 600mg sodium, 300mg potassium.

# Smoky Tempeh Bites

## INGREDIENTS

- 8 oz tempeh, cut into bite-sized cubes
- 1/4 cup soy sauce or tamari
- 2 tablespoons maple syrup
- 2 tablespoons apple cider vinegar
- 1 teaspoon smoked paprika
- 1/2 teaspoon liquid smoke
- 1 tablespoon olive oil
- 1/2 cup vegetable broth or water

 Prep Time: 15 min

Cook Time: 10 minutes

 Serves: 4

## DIRECTIONS

In a bowl, whisk together the soy sauce, maple syrup, apple cider vinegar, smoked paprika, and liquid smoke. Marinate the tempeh cubes in this mixture for at least 10 minutes. Turn on the Instant Pot to Sauté mode and heat the olive oil. Add the marinated tempeh cubes and brown them slightly on all sides.

Add the vegetable broth or water to the Instant Pot, ensuring the tempeh cubes are evenly spread out. Close the Instant Pot lid, set it to Manual or Pressure Cook mode, and cook on high pressure for 5 minutes. Once done, perform a quick release. Serve the smoky tempeh bites warm as an appetizer or as a protein addition to salads, bowls, or wraps.

## NUTRITIONAL INFORMATION

Per serving: 160 calories, 12g protein, 15g carbohydrates, 6g fat, 1g fiber, 0mg cholesterol, 850mg sodium, 300mg potassium.

# Creamy Artichoke Spinach Dip

## INGREDIENTS

- 1 cup raw cashews, soaked for 4 hours and drained
- 1 can (14 oz) artichoke hearts, drained and chopped
- 2 cups fresh spinach, roughly chopped
- 1/2 cup unsweetened almond milk (or any plant-based milk)
- 4 cloves garlic, minced
- 1 tablespoon olive oil
- 1/4 cup nutritional yeast
- 1 lemon, juiced
- 1/2 teaspoon salt
- 1/4 teaspoon black pepper
- 1/4 teaspoon red pepper flakes (optional)

 Prep Time: 10 minutes

 Cook Time: 12 minutes

 Serves: 4

## DIRECTIONS

Turn on the Instant Pot to Sauté mode. Add olive oil and minced garlic, sautéing until fragrant. Add the chopped artichoke hearts and spinach to the pot. Stir occasionally until the spinach is wilted. In a blender, combine the soaked cashews, almond milk, nutritional yeast, lemon juice, salt, and pepper. Blend until smooth. Pour the creamy cashew mixture into the Instant Pot with the artichokes and spinach. Mix well and let the dip heat through for another 3-4 minutes on Sauté mode. Add red pepper flakes if desired for some heat. Serve warm with sliced vegetables, tortilla chips, or crusty bread.

## NUTRITIONAL INFORMATION

Per serving: 230 calories, 9g protein, 18g carbohydrates, 16g fat, 4g fiber, 0mg cholesterol, 480mg sodium, 450mg potassium.

# Instant Pot Guacamole

## INGREDIENTS

- 3 ripe avocados, peeled and pitted
- 1 small red onion, finely diced
- 1-2 cloves garlic, minced
- 1 jalapeño, seeds removed and finely chopped (adjust to taste)
- 1 ripe tomato, seeds removed and diced
- 1 lime, juiced
- 1/4 cup fresh cilantro, chopped
- Salt, to taste
- Freshly ground black pepper, to taste

 Prep Time: 10 min

 Cook Time: 0 minutes

 Serves: 4

## DIRECTIONS

In a bowl, mash the avocados to your desired consistency. Add in the finely diced red onion, minced garlic, chopped jalapeño, and diced tomato. Mix well. Stir in lime juice, chopped cilantro, salt, and black pepper. Adjust seasoning if necessary. For a chilled guacamole, refrigerate for 1 hour before serving. Though it's not traditionally made in the Instant Pot, you can keep your guacamole warm in the Instant Pot using the 'Keep Warm' function if you desire a warm dip. Serve with tortilla chips, veggie sticks, or as a topping for tacos, salads, and other dishes.

## NUTRITIONAL INFORMATION

Per serving: 230 calories, 3g protein, 12g carbohydrates, 20g fat, 9g fiber, 0mg cholesterol, 10mg sodium, 690mg potassium.

# Sweet Potato and Lentil Patties

## INGREDIENTS

- 1 large sweet potato, peeled and diced
- 1 cup dried green or brown lentils, rinsed and drained
- 2 1/2 cups vegetable broth
- 1 small onion, finely chopped
- 2 cloves garlic, minced
- 1 tsp ground cumin
- 1/2 tsp smoked paprika
- 1/4 cup fresh cilantro, chopped
- 1/2 cup breadcrumbs (use gluten-free if necessary)
- Salt and pepper, to taste
- 1 tbsp olive oil (for frying)

 Prep Time: 20 minutes

 Cook Time: 15 minutes

 Serves: 4

## DIRECTIONS

Place the sweet potato, lentils, onion, garlic, and vegetable broth into the Instant Pot. Secure the lid and set the vent to the sealing position. Choose the "Pressure Cook" or "Manual" setting, and set the timer for 10 minutes. Once done, quick-release the pressure. Once the mixture has slightly cooled, drain any excess liquid. Mash the mixture in the pot using a masher or fork until most of the lentils and sweet potatoes are mashed but still have some texture. Mix in cumin, smoked paprika, cilantro, breadcrumbs, salt, and pepper. Shape into patties. On the Instant Pot, set to "Sauté" mode. Add olive oil. Once hot, place the patties in the pot (in batches if necessary) and cook for 2-3 minutes on each side or until golden and crispy. Serve with your favorite vegan sauce or dip.

## NUTRITIONAL INFORMATION

Per serving: 290 calories, 15g protein, 55g carbohydrates, 3g fat, 12g fiber, 0mg cholesterol, 420mg sodium, 650mg potassium.

# Garlic and Herb Breadsticks

## INGREDIENTS

- 2 1/4 tsp (1 packet) active dry yeast
- 1 1/4 cups warm water (110°F)
- 3 1/2 cups all-purpose flour, plus more for dusting
- 2 tbsp olive oil, divided
- 1 tsp sugar
- 1 tsp salt
- 3 cloves garlic, minced
- 2 tbsp fresh herbs (rosemary, thyme, and/or oregano), finely chopped
- 1/2 tsp coarse sea salt (for topping)

  Prep Time: 90 min

 Cook Time: 20 minutes

 Serves: 6

## DIRECTIONS

Dissolve sugar in warm water, add yeast, and let sit until frothy (5-10 mins). Mix flour, 1 tbsp olive oil, and 1 tsp salt in a bowl. Add yeast mixture, stir, and knead on floured surface for 5-7 mins. Let rise for 1 hour. Divide risen dough into 12 parts, shape into breadsticks. Proof in Instant Pot on "Yogurt" setting for 15 mins. Use "Sauté" function, heat 1 tbsp olive oil, sauté garlic and herbs. Brush mixture on breadsticks, sprinkle with sea salt. Without closing the lid, sauté breadsticks in the Instant Pot for 10 mins on each side or until golden brown.

## NUTRITIONAL INFORMATION

Per serving: 230 calories, 6g protein, 45g carbohydrates, 3g fat, 2g fiber, 0mg cholesterol, 400mg sodium, 75mg potassium.

# Steamed Edamame with Lemon Zest

## INGREDIENTS

- 16 oz (about 450g) fresh or frozen edamame in the pod
- 1 cup water
- 2 tsp sea salt, divided
- Zest of 1 lemon
- 1 tbsp olive oil (optional)

 Prep Time: 5 minutes

 Cook Time: 2 minutes

 Serves: 4

## DIRECTIONS

Add 1 cup of water to the Instant Pot. Place a steamer basket or trivet in the pot and add the edamame on top. Close the lid, set the valve to sealing, and set the Instant Pot to "Manual" or "Pressure Cook" on high pressure for 2 minutes. Once done, quick-release the pressure and open the lid. Transfer the edamame to a bowl. While still hot, toss edamame with lemon zest, 1 teaspoon of sea salt, and olive oil if desired.

## NUTRITIONAL INFORMATION

Per serving: 150 calories, 13g protein, 9g carbohydrates, 8g fat, 5g fiber, 0mg cholesterol, 600mg sodium, 500mg potassium.

# Spiced Nut Mix

## INGREDIENTS

- 2 cups mixed nuts (e.g., almonds, cashews, walnuts, pecans)
- 1 tablespoon olive oil
- 1/2 teaspoon smoked paprika
- 1/2 teaspoon ground cumin
- 1/4 teaspoon cayenne pepper (adjust to preference)
- 1/2 teaspoon sea salt
- 1/4 teaspoon black pepper
- 1 tablespoon maple syrup (optional for a hint of sweetness)

 Prep Time: 5 min

 Cook Time: 8 minutes

 Serves: 4

## DIRECTIONS

Turn the Instant Pot on "Sauté" mode and heat olive oil. Once the oil is hot, add the mixed nuts and stir continuously for about 5 minutes until lightly toasted.

Add in the spices (paprika, cumin, cayenne, salt, and black pepper) and continue stirring for an additional 2-3 minutes to coat the nuts evenly with the spice mixture. If desired, stir in the maple syrup for the last minute, ensuring nuts are well-coated. Transfer to a bowl or spread on a tray to cool. Store in an airtight container once cooled.

## NUTRITIONAL INFORMATION

Per serving: 340 calories, 10g protein, 20g carbohydrates, 28g fat, 4g fiber, 0mg cholesterol, 300mg sodium, 400mg potassium.

# Avocado Toast Toppers

## INGREDIENTS

- 2 ripe avocados, peeled and pitted
- 4 slices of whole grain or sourdough bread
- 1 cup cherry tomatoes, halved
- 1 tablespoon olive oil
- 1 garlic clove, minced
- 1/2 teaspoon chili flakes (optional)
- Salt and pepper to taste
- 1 tablespoon lemon juice
- Fresh basil or parsley, chopped for garnish

 Prep Time: 10 minutes

 Cook Time: 5 minutes

 Serves: 4

## DIRECTIONS

Turn the Instant Pot on "Sauté" mode and heat olive oil. Add minced garlic and sauté until fragrant, approximately 1 minute. Add halved cherry tomatoes, chili flakes (if using), salt, and pepper. Sauté for 3-4 minutes until tomatoes are slightly softened. While tomatoes are sautéing, mash the avocados in a bowl, adding lemon juice, salt, and pepper. Toast the bread slices. Spread the mashed avocado evenly on each toasted slice. Top each slice with the tomato mixture from the Instant Pot and garnish with fresh basil or parsley.

## NUTRITIONAL INFORMATION

Per serving: 280 calories, 6g protein, 32g carbohydrates, 15g fat, 8g fiber, 0mg cholesterol, 240mg sodium, 700mg potassium.

# Instant Pot Potato Croquettes

## INGREDIENTS

- 4 medium-sized potatoes, peeled and diced
- 1/2 cup plant-based milk (like almond or soy milk)
- 2 tablespoons vegan butter or olive oil
- Salt and pepper to taste
- 1/2 cup finely chopped green onions
- 1/2 cup breadcrumbs (ensure it's vegan)
- 1 tablespoon nutritional yeast (optional for cheesy flavor)
- 1 teaspoon garlic powder
- 1 teaspoon onion powder
- Olive oil for sautéing

 Prep Time: 15 minutes

 Cook Time: 20 minutes

 Serves: 4

## DIRECTIONS

Add diced potatoes to the Instant Pot along with 1 cup of water. Seal the lid, set the valve to "sealing", and pressure cook on high for 10 minutes. Once done, release the pressure manually and drain any remaining water. Add vegan butter or olive oil, plant-based milk, salt, and pepper. Mash the potatoes until smooth and creamy. Mix in green onions, garlic powder, onion powder, and nutritional yeast (if using) into the mashed potatoes. Form the mixture into small oval-shaped croquettes. Roll each croquette in breadcrumbs until well coated. Set the Instant Pot to "Sauté" mode and add olive oil. Once hot, place the croquettes in the pot and sauté until golden brown on all sides, approximately 3-5 minutes per side.

## NUTRITIONAL INFORMATION

Per serving: 220 calories, 5g protein, 40g carbohydrates, 4g fat, 4g fiber, 0mg cholesterol, 300mg sodium, 750mg potassium.

# Vegan 'Cheese' and Herb Stuffed Mushrooms

## INGREDIENTS

- 16 large button mushrooms, stems removed and finely chopped
- 1 cup vegan cream cheese (store-bought or homemade)
- 2 garlic cloves, minced
- 1/4 cup fresh parsley, finely chopped
- 1/4 cup fresh chives, finely chopped
- 1/4 cup breadcrumbs (ensure it's vegan)
- 1 tablespoon olive oil
- Salt and pepper to taste

Prep Time: 10 minutes

Cook Time: 8 minutes

Serves: 4

## DIRECTIONS

In a bowl, mix chopped mushroom stems, vegan cream cheese, garlic, parsley, chives, salt, and pepper until well combined. Carefully stuff each mushroom cap with the 'cheese' and herb mixture, pressing down slightly to ensure the stuffing is compact. Pour 1 cup of water into the Instant Pot and place the trivet or a steaming basket inside. Arrange the stuffed mushrooms on the trivet or basket. Secure the lid, set the valve to "sealing", and pressure cook on high for 5 minutes. Once done, quick release the pressure. In a pan, heat olive oil over medium heat. Add the stuffed mushrooms and sauté until golden brown on the bottom, about 2-3 minutes.

## NUTRITIONAL INFORMATION

Per serving: 180 calories, 4g protein, 15g carbohydrates, 12g fat, 2g fiber, 0mg cholesterol, 280mg sodium, 380mg potassium.

# Measurement Conversion Charts

## MEASUREMENT

| Cup | Ounces | Milliliters | Tablespoons |
|---|---|---|---|
| 8 cups | 64 oz | 1895 ml | 128 |
| 6 cups | 48 oz | 1420 ml | 96 |
| 5 cups | 40 oz | 1180 ml | 80 |
| 4 cups | 32 oz | 960 ml | 64 |
| 2 cups | 16 oz | 480 ml | 32 |
| 1 cup | 8 oz | 240 ml | 16 |
| 3/4 cup | 6 oz | 177 ml | 12 |
| 2/3 cup | 5 oz | 158 ml | 11 |
| 1/2 cup | 4 oz | 118 ml | 8 |
| 3/8 cup | 3 oz | 90 ml | 6 |
| 1/3 cup | 2.5 oz | 79 ml | 5.5 |
| 1/4 cup | 2 oz | 59 ml | 4 |
| 1/8 cup | 1 oz | 30 ml | 3 |
| 1/16 cup | 1/2 oz | 15 ml | 1 |

## WEIGHT

| Imperial | Metric |
|---|---|
| 1/2 oz | 15 g |
| 1 oz | 29 g |
| 2 oz | 57 g |
| 3 oz | 85 g |
| 4 oz | 113 g |
| 5 oz | 141 g |
| 6 oz | 170 g |
| 8 oz | 227 g |
| 10 oz | 283 g |
| 12 oz | 340 g |
| 13 oz | 369 g |
| 14 oz | 397 g |
| 15 oz | 425 g |
| 1 lb | 453 g |

## TEMPERATURE

| Fahrenheit | Celsius |
|---|---|
| 100 °F | 37 °C |
| 150 °F | 65 °C |
| 200 °F | 93 °C |
| 250 °F | 121 °C |
| 300 °F | 150 °C |
| 325 °F | 160 °C |
| 350 °F | 180 °C |
| 375 °F | 190 °C |
| 400 °F | 200 °C |
| 425 °F | 220 °C |
| 450 °F | 230 °C |
| 500 °F | 260 °C |
| 525 °F | 274 °C |
| 550 °F | 288 °C |

Made in United States
Troutdale, OR
12/23/2024

27189853R00064